# Treasures FROM THE EARTH

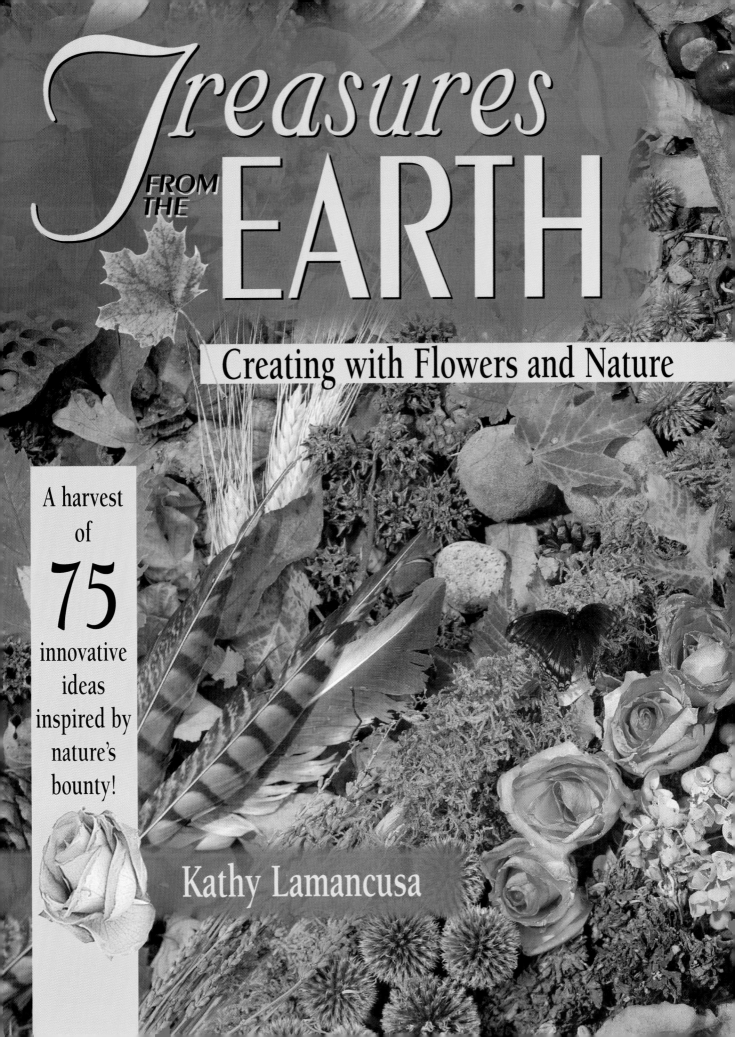

# Treasures FROM THE EARTH

## Creating with Flowers and Nature

A harvest of **75** innovative ideas inspired by nature's bounty!

### Kathy Lamancusa

# krause publications

700 East State St., Iola, WI 54990-0001
Telephone 715-445-2214
www.krause.com

Please call or write for our free catalog of publications. Our toll-free number to place an order or obtain a free catalog is 800-258-0929 or please use our regular business telephone 715-445-2214 for editorial comment and further information.

Photography by Shawn Wood/Studio 7
Book design by Jan Wojtech
Manufactured in the United States of America

Library of Congress Cataloging-In-Publication Data

Lamancusa, Kathy
    Treasures from the earth
    1. title         2. crafts         3. floral crafts

    ISBN 0-87341-561-1
    CIP 97-80619

# ACKNOWLEDGMENTS

**Treasures From The Earth** would not be finished without the help of Katherine Lamancusa and Lydia Huber. Thanks for all your help with project design, project instructions, editing, research and photo styling. I appreciate your many inspirations and creative ideas. You are both very special people.

The stunning photography included in the book was created by Shawn Wood of Studio 7, North Canton, Ohio, with his lovely new bride, Lisa Wood, assisting.

Thanks to the beautiful young ladies whose hands appear in the preparation section of each chapter:
Danielle Soemisch
Stephanie Larkin
Danielle Wood
Anna Wood

Including the use of Kathy and Joe Lamancusa's home, the following families allowed their homes to be used for photography. Thank you for allowing us to tramp, trail, and display the projects throughout your beautiful homes.
Scott and Susie Jackson
Norman and Carole Jackson
Laura and Anthony Magistro
Lisa and Shawn Wood

The following companies provided many of the beautiful products used in this book:

Artisan Spirit
Dremel
Knud Nielsen
International Flower Imports
Rhyne Floral Supply
Syndicate Sales
Smithers Oasis
Design Master color tool, Inc.
Winter Woods
Wright's

C.M. Offray & Son Ribbon
Lion Ribbon Company
Walnut Hollow
Windflower Farms
Universal Sunray
American Oak Preserving
  Company
Florasense by Endar
Fiskars
Dow Chemical

# TABLE OF CONTENTS

## PART ONE
# SHELLS

## PART TWO
# BIRDS & BUTTERFLIES

## PART THREE
# NATURE

# DEDICATION

I dedicate this book to my husband, Joe, who is truly a treasure. Thanks for all of your help, guidance and support.

Your attention to detail, while I look at the big picture, allowed the completion of this book to be on time and within budget!

All my love to you — forever!

# INTRODUCTION

The title for this book came to me one day as I was walking through the woods. The bright sunshine filtered through breaks in the trees and played on the ground. The area was alive with shapes, smells, textures and colors. I began to think of the treasures in the woods and all of nature with its beautiful flowers, rugged stones and bountiful harvests.

I grew up surrounded by flowers and nature. Flowers have always held a special place in my heart. My grandparents were avid gardeners and filled their yard with multitudes of flowers of every size, shape and color. I spent many an afternoon helping to water, weed and plant.

Flowers are stress-relievers and provide a moment of calm in our hectic lives. My dear friend Lee Robert believes flowers are like Angels from heaven and are truly a gift of God.

I wish I could bring each of you for a visit to the set of our popular television show, *At Home With Flowers*. The prep room is overflowing with flowers and items from nature. These items are provided by family, friends, and growers around the world. My guests arrive and spend hours and hours preparing their designs. The days of shooting are long, but everyone involved with our show remains upbeat and happy. I think the reason the stress does not "get to them" the way it might on a regular television show is because they are surrounded by so many beautiful materials. I have seen camera operators or sound directors stop and take an extra whiff of a bucket of roses or freesia. Our days are full of breathtaking sights and fragrances.

You too can surround yourself with beautiful materials. I have designed the projects in this book for you — so you can experience the wonder of nature. Each project is easy to create with materials that should be easy to find. If, however, you have trouble finding a particular product in your area of the country, substitute something that is similar in size, shape and color.

As you work your way through the book, try not to "just make projects." Try to create experiences as well. Take a walk in the woods and/or plant some herbs and flowers. Look for treasures around every corner and under every bush and tree.

**Treasures From The Earth** is about creating designs and the journey through the garden of life. This book is about making flowers and natural materials an integral part of your home and lifestyle. Take a few moments to be still. Experience the beauty that surrounds you in a way that will truly nurture your spirit.

*Kathy Lamancusa*

# PART ONE
## Shells

You may already have a collection of seashells from your childhood. Most of us can find a box, can, or bag filled with treasures that we tucked away many years ago. These treasures serve as a reminder of a jaunt along the sandy shores of the beach. Seashells are hard to resist. They are truly one of nature's wonders. As we study their form, shape, pattern, and color we can clearly see that each is a marvel. Summer beaches are full of seashells in many sizes, shapes, and color variations. Capture the tantalizing tang of the sea by searching for sea lavender, dried seaweed, scraps of discarded rope, and decorative materials that may be craggy and rugged as well as pearly and elegant. Unfortunately, after a vacation we often tuck away the materials from the beach and quickly forget them. Now is the time to dig them out and use their subtle beauty to create spectacular natural decorations for your home.

When I was a child, I sat for hours by the edge of the water as the waves came rolling in, bringing with them many wonderful treasures from the sea. I remember being intrigued every time I watched a wave roll back out to sea. As the wave eroded the surface of the sand it revealed hundreds of tiny shells. I was not sure why, but within seconds, these tiny shells disappeared under the surface of the sand. I recall thinking the shells were incredibly beautiful.

I remember grabbing a handful of these "disappearing" shells as the waves rolled back, before they had a chance to bury themselves again. As I held them, to my surprise I immediately felt tiny movements in the palm of my hand. I screamed and dropped the whole handful! As I watched, they quickly buried themselves in the sand again. I then learned that tiny animals lived in those shells. The shells I picked up were still homes and I had just disturbed them!

Most of the shells we find are empty. However, be careful not to disturb those that are being used as homes. Whether you find your treasures on the beach or buy them from a shell or crafts retailer, the special uniqueness of each will help you create one-of-a-kind gifts and decorations.

Do you have memories of collecting shells, walking on the beach, and being lost in the sound of the waves? During the hectic times in your life, recollect these memories. Your thoughts will be calming and comforting.

# FINDING AND PREPARING THE TREASURE

Some areas of the United States and some foreign countries prohibit the removal of shells from the beach. Learn the rules of the area before selecting treasures to take home. You can also search for shells in places other than the beach. Fish vendors supply pickings of shells such as mussels, oysters, scallops, and clams. Turn these into fabulous gifts and use them in home decorating. There are numerous shops along the waterfront that also supply a wide selection of shells that are difficult to find individually on the beach. Also check out your local craft or supply shop. They can often order what you need.

If you find shells on the beach, clean them before storage. Wash each one with warm water to get rid of any salty deposits. Most shells only require rinsing or perhaps brushing with an old toothbrush. Shells are very fragile and can crack or chip when rubbed against each other. Be careful as you clean and store them. Some shells will have a crust or scale. Scrape and chip this crust away. Be careful not to remove any of the natural coating or weathering. In many cases the crusting gives the shells added character and causes them to look less perfect and more natural.

If the shell you find is the home of a live specimen that has died, the soft parts will require removal. Remove parts by putting the shell into a saucepan of cold water and bring to a boil. Boil for ten minutes. Allow the pan to cool naturally and remove the cleaned shell. Rinse the shell before using.

Gifts made with seashells are often very special. My sister loves the sea and anything that reminds her of it. She will often buy small gifts for me that contain shells or that have a shell motif involved in the construction.

While spending several weeks in the hospital with my son, who was severely injured in an automobile accident, my sister brought a wonderful gift to me. It was a stitchery kit that featured a collection of shells. The colors were soft and delicate and the design was exquisite in its simplicity. I did not begin to sew the design while in the hospital. I slept on a cot next to my son's bed and placed the kit beside the cot. My eyes frequently wandered to that picture during the long days and nights of caring for my son. During these times, my mind would visit the beach. Within my mind I heard the waves crashing. I envisioned the shells covering the beach. I imagined the wind and sun on my face. These pleasant respites helped me to handle the difficult situations during the long days of recovery. In my imagination, I communed with nature and it was refreshing and comforting.

# SHELL CANDLES

Candles add a special warmth. I love to sit in a hot bubble bath with only the light of a candle to fill the room. After a long day, stress just melts away under the warm glow of the candlelight. Shells are great containers for these relaxing lights.

Shells are also naturally brilliant candleholders for a dinner party. They provide a warm glow close to any area of a table. Never leave candles to burn unattended. For safety, place them on a heat-resistant surface.

Shell candles are made quickly and easily in one of two ways. Both will produce similar results. The first is the traditional method of melting wax and suspending a wick in the center of the candle. The second and more current method is to pour granulated wax into the container. Insert a pre-waxed wick into the wax. Place the candle in the oven or under a strong hot light and allow the granules to melt. The wax will cool to form a solid candle.

## COLLECTING SUPPLIES FOR THE TRADITIONAL WAX-MELTING METHOD:

*Deep scallop, clam, or cockle shells*
*Smaller scallop, clam, or cockle shells for*
*    bases*
*Sheets of wax*
*Cotton wicking*
*Wooden skewer*
*Putty or wick base*
*Candle scent or candle color, if desired*
*Silicone glue*

## CREATING THE DESIGN:

Glue a slightly smaller shell upside-down as a base for a larger shell. Be sure the base acts as a leveling tool for the candle shell. Doing so will prevent wax from pouring over the sides when added.

Never use hot glue for this application. As the lighted candle gets hot, it can melt the glue and cause the shells to separate.

Cut a length of wick that will extend from the bottom of the shell to approximately 1″ (2.5cm) above the top of the potential level of wax. Tie the end of the wicking to the center of the wooden skewer. Place the wooden skewer on top of the edges of the shell. Using the putty or wick base, secure the other end of the wicking to the bottom center of the shell. Melt the wax in an old pan and, if desired, add small amounts of candle color or candle scent. Pour melted wax into the shell surrounding the wick. When the wax is cool, cut the wick away from the skewer.

## COLLECTING SUPPLIES FOR CANDLES WITH GRANULATED WAX:

*Shells*
*Granulated wax*
*Wax-coated wicking*
*Hot lamp or broiler*

## CREATING THE DESIGN:

Pour granulated wax into the shell. Granulated wax is available in a variety of colors. Cut the length of wax-coated wicking so that it extends above the level of granulated wax. Insert this wick into the center of the shell. Place the shell under the broiler or lamp until the wax melts. The candle will form when the wax cools. If you wish, use the candle without first melting the wax. The granules melt as the wick burns.

*Right: The warm glow of candlelight from the Shell Candles enhances the beauty of Glass Memory Balls and a Decorated Starfish.*

## GREAT IDEA!

Create a clay saucer candle following the directions for the shell candles using a clay saucer for your base. After pouring the wax and while it is starting to cool, place a collection of shells, starfish, and other sea inspired items around the outside edge of the saucer. Gently press them into the wax to hold securely.

# DECORATED STARFISH

Starfish are incredibly beautiful treasures from the sea. They are unique in that they are found in all sizes and each one dries in a slightly different way. The wonderful story that follows is often shared by professional speakers. The story involves an older man, a young boy, and a starfish. I have heard several versions of this story, each with slightly different characters. In each version the starfish always remains the important element of the story. My sons, Joe and Jim, have chosen to include the story in their professional speeches that challenge students to set goals and motivate themselves to success. I share this story with you:

*An old man was walking along the beach one day and saw a young boy reach down, pick something up and throw it back into the ocean. Curious, the man walked toward the boy to see what he was doing. As he approached the boy, he saw that the beach was covered with starfish. The starfish had washed up on shore and could not make it back into the ocean. The old man asked the young boy what he was doing. "Throwing starfish back into the ocean," the boy responded, "because if I don't, they will die."*

*As he looked at the many starfish on the beach, the astonished old man replied, "How can you ever expect to make a difference? There are so many starfish on this beach." The young boy briefly glanced at the old man and without saying a word, reached down, picked up another starfish and threw it out into the ocean. "It makes a difference to that one."*

Make a difference in the life of someone you love. Share this special gift with them.

## COLLECTING SUPPLIES:

*One starfish approximately 5" across (12.7cm)*
*Three assorted shells approximately 1-1/2" long (3.8cm)*
*1 yard (.91cm) of 3/4" (1.9cm) wide mesh ribbon*
*1-1/4 yard (1.14m) of 1/8" (.3cm) double face satin ribbon*
*Two lengths raffia*
*Small bunch dried flowers*
*A few small berries*
*Cloth covered wire*
*Glue*

## CREATING THE DESIGN:

Begin by forming the hanging loop from 1/4 yard (22.9cm) of the double faced satin ribbon. Form the ribbon into a loop by bringing the ends together, then glue the ends behind one of the tips of the starfish. Before turning it over, allow it to dry.

With the mesh ribbon, form a bow that does not have a center loop and secure it with cloth covered wire. Form additional bows without center loops using one yard (.91cm) of the double faced satin ribbon and the raffia. Secure with wire. Glue all three bows into the center of the starfish.

Glue the small seashells into the bow loops. Cluster a group of dried materials and glue them in the center of the bows. Cut the stems of the berries short and glue the berries into the design between the shells.

Coordinate the colors of ribbons, berries, dried materials, and shells to achieve a pleasing look. Hang this elegant design in an extra-special place on the wall. Make multiple designs using holiday colors.

Decorated starfish make spectacular Christmas tree decorations. If you are unable to share the starfish story in person, write it on a piece of parchment. Roll up the parchment and attach it to the starfish through a small circle of ribbon glued to the back of the design.

# GLASS MEMORY BALLS

These clear, glass balls are reminders of the ocean and are very easy to make. They are wonderful gifts and encourage the receiver to remember happy times spent at the beach. As you hold the ball in your hand, the sand and seashells swirl around inside and add an extra tactile element that gives more value and pleasure. Make several of these visually compelling balls in various sizes. Hang them from lengths of raffia in a window where they can catch and reflect the sunlight. To add visual interest to a room, place a collection of balls in a large, deep bowl and display on a table. Decorate a Christmas tree. Create an additional gift and incorporate a ball in the bow on a package. Remember a vacation excursion and create this project with sand and shells collected from the beach.

*After pouring sand and placing shells into the clear glass ornament balls, decorate the top with raffia and other decorative shells.*

## COLLECTING SUPPLIES:

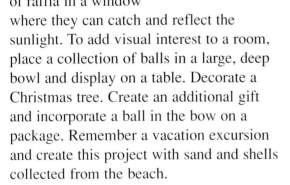

*One clear glass Christmas ornament ball
    with a removable cap*
*White sand*
*Small seashells that will fit through the
    opening of the ball*
*Two or three lengths of raffia*
*A few larger shells, starfish, or seahorse*
*Glue*

## CREATING THE DESIGN:

Remove the cap and pour enough sand to fill 1/3 to 1/2 of the inside of the ball. Drop several small shells into the ball. Add as many shells as you wish. Replace the cap. Tie a bow around the cap of the ball with lengths of raffia. Glue the accent shells on top of the bow, covering the front of the cap of the ball. Leave the hook on the cap free and use it to hang.

# VINE WREATH WITH SHELLS

**A** striking appearance is created with a combination of the deep, rough texture of the vine wreath and the smooth texture of the shells. The image of shells washed up on the beach inspired this design. I created this wreath to coordinate with the soft and soothing colors of the bathroom. A skylight and the beauty of green plants complete the decor of the room.

## COLLECTING SUPPLIES:

One 18" (45.7cm) bleached vine wreath
Peach floral color spray
Glitter gold floral spray
30-40 assorted seashells and four large
    decorative starfish, approximately
    4" to  6" (10.2cm to 15.2cm)
1-1/2 yards (1.37m) 3" (7.6cm) wide
    natural mesh ribbon
Two stems natural Indian potter grass
Three lengths green preserved running
    cedar
Spanish moss
30 gauge cloth covered wire
Glue

## CREATING THE DESIGN:

Spray the wreath sparingly with the peach floral color and allow to dry. When spraying, hold the can 12 to 18 inches (30.5cm to 45.7cm) away from the vine wreath and apply with short quick bursts. This will create a textured effect that has a great deal of depth. Continue to use this spraying technique until you are happy with the coverage. Lightly spray the wreath with gold glitter. Allow the wreath to dry completely.

Loop and drape the ribbon around the wreath. Gather and secure with the shorter lengths of the cloth covered wire at various points. Secure the ends of the ribbon at the back of the wreath with glue.

Glue small sections of moss around the wreath. On the bottom of the wreath, glue the assortment of shells in a crescent shape.

*The bath is the perfect location to display projects created from shells and natural materials.*

Weave and glue small amounts of greenery between the shells. Break the branches into short lengths and glue them between the shells.

Add special shells such as starfish, seahorse, and sand dollars for interest.

*A Vine Wreath with Shells creates a focal point for Shell Soaps, a Bath Scrub, and a candle created in a clay saucer.*

# SHELL SOAP

**H**andmade soap, formed as a shell, is a wonderful gift. You may love these so much you will want to make several to add beauty to your own bathroom.

## COLLECTING SUPPLIES:

*One bar of unscented soap*
*Grater*
*Few drops of boiling water*
*Assorted size clam shells*
*Bowl*

## CREATING THE DESIGN:

Add a few teaspoons of boiling water to soap you have grated into the bowl. To make it soft and easy to mold, mix the hot water into the soap. After the soap has softened, put it into the clam shell. Firmly press it down with your fingers so it shapes and conforms to the shell. Pack the shells solid with soap. After the soap has cooled, remove it from the shell. To hasten the set up time, place soap filled shells in the freezer and leave them for approximately 60 to 90 minutes.

Use powdered turmeric to produce a golden to orange color or paprika for a peach colored shell. Use the spices sparingly.

Add oatmeal, ground lemon or orange peel, cornmeal, cinnamon, ginger, ground cloves, powdered kelp, and essential oils for added textures and fragrances.

*After mixing the soap, press it firmly into a deep scallop shell.*

## GREAT IDEA!

Enhance this gift by placing the shell soap on top of a washcloth or hand towel. Tie together with a length of natural string or gold ribbon. Glue a few shells to the ends of the string or ribbon. Extra pieces of raffia add a finishing touch when tied into the bow.

# BATH SCRUB

The color tones of this mixture make it so appealing it demands display. Fill a glass container with this stimulating bath scrub and use it as a housewarming gift for a special friend or relative. Decorate the container with ribbon, raffia, or tassels to coordinate with the decor of the bath. Embellish with a small cluster of shells.

## COLLECTING SUPPLIES:

*5 cups oatmeal*
*1 cup dried thyme*
*1 cup scented dried red rosebuds*
*Grated orange peel from two oranges*
*Small grinder*
*Airtight storage container of your choice, a glass container will best feature the scrub's beautiful coloration*

*Ground oatmeal, thyme, rosebuds, and oranges combine to form a healthful and beautifying bath scrub.*

## CREATING THE MIXTURE:

Grind each ingredient separately in a small grinder, then mix everything together well in a large bowl. Pour the mixture into an airtight container. Include a small wooden scoop or clam shell to use for measuring out the scrub.

To use, rub a small amount on damp skin, then rinse. Keep the mixture stored in an airtight container away from strong heat and light.

The oatmeal soothes and smoothes. The rosebuds and orange peel are for fragrance. The thyme refreshes and revitalizes.

*Display the hidden beauty of sand dollars in a frame and make a coordinated wreath and trinket box to showcase your favorite shells.*

# SHELL TRINKET BOX

Store treasures collected from vacation trips or other memorabilia in this sea-inspired trinket box. The beauty of this box enhances the desk of a gentleman or the dressing area of a lady.

## COLLECTING SUPPLIES:

*One 9" x 7" (22.9cm x 17.8cm) oval or 7"*
*(17.8cm) round papier mache' box*
*with a lid*
*A collection of smaller shells,*
*approximately 70-100*
*A few larger, decorative shells,*
*approximately 8-10*
*Sand*
*Sponge brush*
*Acrylic paint to match color of sand*
*Spanish moss*
*Reddish brown preserved salignum*
*Craft stick*
*Thick white glue*

## CREATING THE DESIGN:

Paint the inside and outside of both the box and lid. Allow to dry.

In a disposable bowl, create a mixture that is easy to spread by combining equal parts of glue and sand. Set the lid aside. Coat the outside of the bottom of the box with the mixture, spreading evenly with a craft stick. Paint one side of the box at a time. Sprinkle additional sand over the mixture while still tacky. Tap off excess sand. Allow to dry. Glue pieces of salignum around the middle.

*Combine sand and white glue to create a textured covering.*

Glue a light covering of Spanish moss firmly to the top of the lid. Glue shells closely together onto the moss covered lid. Add tiny bits of salignum between the shells.

*A craft stick is useful to apply the mixture of sand and glue.*

Glue the larger, decorative items such as starfish, old pearls, and sea coral to the center top of the box lid.

## GREAT IDEA!

Create small trinket boxes by attaching hinges to large scallop shells. Wash and dry the two halves of the shell. Sand the area inside the shell ends where the hinge will go. This will provide more tooth to the area and allow glue to work well and eliminate sliding.

Glue one side of the hinge inside the base of the shell and allow to completely dry. Glue the other side in place on the other shell and allow the glue to dry completely before flexing the hinge. Be careful not to get glue on the hinge area.

Embellish this delightful little box by gluing tiny feathers, loops of leather cording, small seashells, or tiny pieces of sea coral to the top of the shell.

# SHELL MIRROR FRAME

**T**his beautifully framed mirror is a welcome addition to any home decor setting. It is quite easy to make and truly displays the many treasures you find along the beach. It is also a spectacular table centerpiece. Another idea is to center a group of votive candles on top of the mirror. Light the candles and watch the flickering reflection in the mirror.

## COLLECTING SUPPLIES:

*Round mirror with foam frame, mirror measures 14" (35.6cm), frame is 17" (43.2cm) ***
*Assorted seashells, some smaller and uniform in size and shape, some larger, unique shapes for accent. Broken pieces look great combined in this design. You will need 200-300 shells.*
*1 lb. preserved green baby eucalyptus*
*Six 4" (10.2cm) dried mini palms*
*1 package dried oats*
*2 oz. sheet moss*
*50-60 floral pins*
*3 yards 5/8" (1.6cm) wide cream satin ribbon*
*2 oz. raffia*
*Whitewash spray color*
*Glue*

*\* If a mirror with a foam frame attached is not available, make one yourself. Attach a mirror to the back of a half round foam wreath with glue and heavy pins.*

## CREATING THE DESIGN:

Spray eucalyptus with whitewash. Allow the natural color to show. Allow to dry. Break eucalyptus stems into clusters of three to four pieces, 4" to 5" (10.2cm to 12.7cm) long. Use floral pins to attach clusters of eucalyptus all around the mirror, covering the foam base.

Glue the shells closely together around the wreath. Glue tufts of sheet moss, dried oats, and the mini palms between the shells. Crinkle the ribbon in your hand. Wind the ribbon and raffia loosely around and through the shells and eucalyptus, randomly gluing or pinning to hold in place.

## GREAT IDEA!

Use other spray colors to lightly mist eucalyptus and ribbon. Coordinate with your home decor color scheme.

# SAND DOLLAR SHADOW BOX

The sand dollar is one of nature's most unusual shells. Notice the intricacies on the front and back of the shell. The following verse beautifully articulates the symbolic importance of sand dollars.

### THE SAND DOLLAR
*The five slits in the shell represent the five wounds in the body of Christ.*
*The Star of Bethlehem, a five pointed star, is in the center front of the Easter Lily design.*
*Notice the outline of a Poinsettia, the Christmas flower, on the back. Upon opening the shell, you will find five perfectly formed replicas of a dove. These are the Doves of Peace.*

The words can be hand-printed or done in calligraphy. Another option is to produce words on a home computer and print them on parchment paper. Display these in the shadow box.

## COLLECTING SUPPLIES:

*An assortment of smaller shells and sand dollars, approximately 30*
*9" x 11" shadow box frame (22.9cm x 27.9cm)*
*4" x 3-1/2" printed verse (10.2cm x 8.9cm)*
*Mat board sized to fit the back of the shadow box*
*White sand*
*Tiny chisel and hammer or X-Acto™ knife*
*Thick white glue*
*Craft stick*
*Acrylic paint to match the color of the sand*
*Sponge brush*

## CREATING THE DESIGN:

Paint the mat board and allow to dry. Mix equal parts white glue and sand together in a disposable container to form a mixture that is easy to spread. Coat the entire surface of the mat board with this mixture. Sprinkle a small amount of sand over the glue mixture and allow to dry. Tap off excess sand.

*Insert shells into a heavy mixture of sand and glue to portray finding shells in the sand.*

Mix a second batch of sand and glue, but this time use at least twice as much sand as glue. The mixture should be very thick. Form a mound of the glue and sand mixture at the upper left and lower left corners of the mat board. Spread the mixture with a craft stick to simulate a washed beach. Randomly cluster shells, sand dollars, and tiny pieces of greenery into each of the sand mounds. The shells will look as if they are embedded in the sand on the beach. Sprinkle sand over the mounded shells and allow to dry. Tap off excess sand. Be sure that you leave enough edge around the mat board to glue it into the back of the frame.

Carefully tear around the verse. Using a lighted match, char the edges of the paper around the poem. Do only a small portion at a time. Glue the verse near the top right corner of the mat board.

Cut open a large sand dollar by inserting the sharp point of an X-Acto™ knife into the center of the sand dollar and gently cutting through half of the shell, then pulling apart to separate. Gently remove the doves. Place the two halves of the broken sand dollar slightly separated and glue in place at the lower right corner. Glue the five doves extending upward toward the verse with the largest doves closest to the opened shell.

# SHELL TOPIARY

**S**hell covered containers have a special meaning to the Lamancusa family. My husband's grandfather (Nannu, as he was known to us) made dozens of them during his retirement years. Nannu and Nanna loved to pick shells off the beach in Florida during the winter months. During the summer, Nannu used a thickened mortar mixture and spread it over a large garden-sized clay pot. He then pushed shells deeply into the mortar and allowed it to dry. The look was spectacular! I am sure that every family member received at least one during the years Nannu was with us. Created 35-40 years ago, many are still beautiful today. I think back to the care Nannu took to make each one unique and different. I often wish that we had more of his handwork to display in our home.

I have used one of these "Nannu original" pots to create a topiary design. This is a wonderful display on a deck, patio, or in a sunroom.

*The beauty of a topiary made with seashells is enhanced even more when created in an heirloom container.*

If you like, you can experience the beauty of this technique by making a smaller version of the design using thick glue instead of mortar.

Dirt

Gravel

Foam

## COLLECTING SUPPLIES:

*One clay pot*
*Shells of assorted size and shape. You'll*
*    need a few hundred*
*Mortar or thick craft glue*
*Styrofoam® or dry floral foam*
*Foam ball in proportion to the size of*
*    the pot*
*Moss green floral color spray*
*Birch branches to form trunk*
*Raffia*
*Lycopodium or other preserved greenery*
*Small fresh plants*
*Potting soil*
*Wooden picks*
*24 gauge wire*
*Floral pins*

## CREATING THE DESIGN:

Exact dimensions are not provided for this project. Custom create it to fit the preferred location of display. Purchase materials such as the ball, pot, and trunk, that are in proportion to each other. When choosing the ball, remember to visualize the size of the finished design which is several inches larger than the ball.

Begin by spreading a very thick coat of mortar over the outside of the clay pot. Press assorted shells firmly into the mortar, placing them as close together as possible. Allow to dry before moving.

Spray the foam ball with a moss green floral color. Cut birch branches to the desired length and bind them together with wire to form the trunk. Insert the trunk into the covered foam ball and glue. Use floral pins to entirely cover the ball with lycopodium or other preserved greenery.

Wedge or glue a block of Styrofoam® or dry floral foam at the bottom of the pot. It should be approximately 1/3 the height of the pot and it should fit tightly. Glue the base of the trunk into the foam. Sprinkle a one inch layer of gravel over the foam. Fill the remainder of the pot with potting soil. Plant fresh plants.

Glue the shells to the wooden picks and insert into the foam ball. Loop and drape the lengths of raffia between the shells using floral pins to hold them in place. Allow some of the raffia to drape from the ball.

## GREAT IDEA!

Display three or four coordinating topiaries together. If desired, use a cone shaped foam base in place of the ball shape. For your topiary, you may prefer to leave the trunk longer and use two balls or a ball and cone.

✤ Wet shells have a spectacular variety of color. When shells dry, this natural beauty fades. To display shells and reveal this underwater magic, simply fill large glass storage jars with shells and add distilled water.

✤ To help shells keep their brilliance when dry, apply a thin coat of varnish to each shell or spray with a thick gloss sealer. Be sure shells are completely dry before moving or using in a design.

✤ As an attractive alternative for displaying slightly larger shells, use miniature shelves and old printer's cases. Using spray adhesive, apply felt or fabric to the back of the compartments. Glue the shells in place.

✤ Make pale shells more interesting by painting with thin watercolors. Brush the color sparingly over the surface. To add a pastel glow, finish each shell by applying a coat of varnish or thick spray gloss sealer.

If you wish to add a permanent subtle color to shell work designs that will be displayed outdoors, use metallic car paints. Coat with an outdoor varnish as well.

✤ Shell jewelry is easy to make and fun to wear. Purchase plain jewelry bases such as hairclips, headbands, and earring findings. Use a craft cement to glue shells to the bases. Try mixing colors, textures, and sizes of shells.

✤ To emphasize a variety of colors and patterns, display sea-washed shells and pebbles in a plain dish. This becomes a tactile decoration. Guests find it irresistible and will constantly rearrange and handle the materials. This is a fun, stress-reducing display.

✤ Make an unusual potpourri with a variety of tiny shells. Place a collection of shells into a lidded container and add two to three drops of essential oil. The scent you select can have a heady aroma such as sandalwood or cloves, a refreshing scent such as lemon or eucalyptus, or the sweet smell of lavender or rose oil. Leave these in the tightly lidded container for at least one week. Then display in a large scallop shell or small decorative saucer.

✤ The fascinating shapes, variety of textures, and subtlety of color represented in shells are perfect when used to accent a curtain. Simply glue a collection of shells to roped tiebacks. Carry the look through by placing larger, more decorative shells along the window ledges in the same room.

✤ Add citronella essential oil to candle wax before pouring into the shells for insect-repellent characteristics. These candles are ideal for use on warm summer nights. Place at each table setting or scatter them generously around the deck.

# PART TWO
# Birds and Butterflies

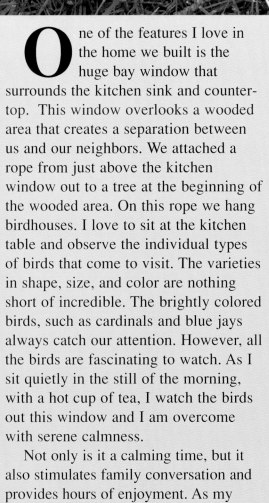

One of the features I love in the home we built is the huge bay window that surrounds the kitchen sink and countertop. This window overlooks a wooded area that creates a separation between us and our neighbors. We attached a rope from just above the kitchen window out to a tree at the beginning of the wooded area. On this rope we hang birdhouses. I love to sit at the kitchen table and observe the individual types of birds that come to visit. The varieties in shape, size, and color are nothing short of incredible. The brightly colored birds, such as cardinals and blue jays always catch our attention. However, all the birds are fascinating to watch. As I sit quietly in the still of the morning, with a hot cup of tea, I watch the birds out this window and I am overcome with serene calmness.

Not only is it a calming time, but it also stimulates family conversation and provides hours of enjoyment. As my sons were growing up we often watched the birds. We tried to decide what types of birds were at our "restaurant" that day. We bought books that identified birds, discussed the variety of feeding options, and decided which menu items would attract which type of bird. We watched each spring to see where the first birds decided to make their homes. Numerous trees surround our house so we never knew which the birds would decide to use!

For several years a family of robins decided to build their home in the tree directly outside my son Jim's bedroom window. During the summers, Jim did not need an alarm clock. The birds awakened him with their early morning chirping. I knew they had been especially rambunctious on several mornings when I discovered him with a pillow over his head and his bedroom windows closed — when the outside temperature was in the 80s!

Occasionally we found tiny birds that had fallen from their nests. Our hope was always to save one of these birds and one day let them loose into their natural habitat. Sadly, we were never that fortunate.

Collecting the used nests at the end of the season is always fun. Sometimes we find unhatched eggs inside and try to identify the type of birds that had lived in the nest. The birds are not always careful about where they build their nests. My sister had a bird family build a nest in the wreath on her front door. We were all surprised at this because the front door was often used by the family. When the nest was in place, the birds did not want to move. They chirped loudly when disturbed, but continued to live there throughout the season.

Because of the woods surrounding our home, we do not have enough sunny areas to grow many flowers. Fortunately however, we occasionally find butterflies who decide to move in for a season.

We have the opportunity to visit several public gardens where the butterflies are plentiful. I am fascinated by the way they appear to float on the air…I wish I could do the same!

# CREATING A NURTURING HAVEN

## BIRDS

Encourage birds to visit your yard by providing their three basic needs: food, shelter, and water. Continue to provide for them through all the seasons. During the winter days, birds need a constant source of food so that they do not freeze at night. Since seeds have not yet developed, natural foods are scarce during the spring. Food is more readily available during the summer months, however as eggs continue to hatch there are more birds that require feeding. Do not miss watching adult birds bring their young to familiar feeding spots.

During the fall and winter, attract birds with viburnums, bittersweet, cotoneaster, crabapples, honeysuckle, holly, and juniper. Elderberry, black cherry, white flowering dogwood, red twig dogwood, blueberry, blackberry, mulberry, and spice bushes produce summer fruits and berries our feathered friends will enjoy.

Most species have preferred food and are comfortable eating in certain places. Meat eaters eat vegetables as well as worms and insects. Migratory birds seek high-fat fruits and seeds for extra energy during their journey. Winter birds eat more to maintain warmth in their bodies. Vegetarians will hunt insects and worms when feeding their young.

To attract cardinals, I supply oil-type sunflower, striped sunflower, cracked corn, and safflower seeds. In addition to these, blue jays also eat bread and peanuts. If you add thistles, finches will join the party. Suet attracts woodpeckers, starlings, nuthatches, and some mockingbirds.

Hummingbirds are one of my favorite birds. I love the way their bodies reflect the light. As they hover delicately in the air, they appear to be little fairies. The best way to attract them is with plants that are profusely covered with sweet nectar flowers.

To entice these delicate creatures, plant the following in your garden: butterfly bush, hibiscus, azalea, weigela, honeysuckle, hollyhocks, columbine, fuschia, impatiens, salvia, and phlox. A commercial hummingbird feeder is also effective if placed away from people and yard traffic. Hummingbirds love to use the fuzz from pussy willow branches to build their nests. They also love to perch on trellises.

The food you choose to put out for the birds may attract pesky visitors, such as squirrels. Distract these visitors by providing acorns, nuts, and corn cobs. Place food quite a distance away from the bird feeder.

Furnish shelter by planting flowers, shrubs, and trees. Shelters include ground cover, birdhouses, or tall shade trees. They provide nesting places, feed, and protection from weather and predators.

All birds need water to drink and a place to bathe. Provide fresh, clean water to eliminate their need to fly off in search of this essential. In the winter, break the ice on bird baths to assure that winter birds have access to water.

## BUTTERFLIES

Butterflies love color and fragrance. Colorful perennials and nectar producing shrubs are their favorites. No two butterfly gardens are the same and none are typical. One gardener may choose to use a window box filled with daisies and alyssum. Another may plant a meadow filled with black-eyed Susans and a colorful array of wildflowers. To entice butterflies to perch, place beautiful potted

plants and window boxes near a fence.

Butterflies are most active in sunny areas. A very slow moving water source that is close to the ground will also attract butterflies. They cannot drink from an open body of water such as a lake.

The most popular plants used to lure butterflies are butterfly bush, spicebush, spiraea, and orange milkweed (butterfly weed). These plants work extremely well for the following:

**For color** — fuschia, phlox, daisies, asters, goldenrod, Joe-Pye weed, yarrow, marigolds, zinnias, sedum, liatris, lobelia, and verbena.

**For fragrance** — heliotrope, sweet William, lilac, lavender, sweet alyssum, and viburnum.

To attract more butterflies, plan your garden so that selected flowers are in full bloom at different times of the season.

# BIRD FEEDER FEAST

**T**his is a project the entire family will enjoy creating and maintaining. It is the natural rustic look that attracts many types of birds. It holds several varieties of food — seeds, nuts, millet, and tasty bird seed balls. It's almost like a smorgasbord restaurant!

## COLLECTING SUPPLIES:

### FOR THE WREATH:

One 18" (45.7cm) grapevine wreath
20" x 20" (50.8cm x 50.8cm) soft wire
   mesh screening
Sheet moss
Peanuts in their shells
Millet
Bird Seed
4 to 6 yards (3.66m to 5.49m) 1-1/2"
   (3.8cm) wide green burlap strips
Staple gun
Nylon fishing line
Large needle

### FOR BIRDSEED BALLS:

One cup peanut butter
Four cups cornmeal
One cup shortening or lard
One cup white flour
Chicken wire

### FOR MINI BIRDHOUSES:

9" (22.9cm) long x 1-1/2" (3.8cm)
   diameter birch branch
24" (61cm) long x 1/4" (.6cm) diameter
   dowel rod
13-1/2" (34.3cm) long x 2-1/4" (5.7cm)
   wide x 1/4" (.6cm) thick plywood
   board
Wood glue
Small hand saw
Drill with 3/4" (1.9cm) bit and 1/4"
   (.6cm) bit
Small finishing nails
Hammer

*Birds and butterflies will be attracted to this area of your yard for the color, food, fragrances, and water.*

## CREATING THE WREATH DESIGN:

Cut four burlap strips to the length that will best fit the area where the bird feeder is to hang. Wire and glue each end equally spaced around the inside of the wreath and tie the other ends to an overhanging branch or clothesline.

Cut the screening to fit inside the wreath, allowing extra space. This extra space creates a generous pouch in the center of the wreath. Use a staple gun to secure it in place. If the grapevine wreath is formed with narrow

*Staple the screening inside the grapevine wreath. Use wire to attach it if extra support is needed.*

*Cut the ends of a birch branch into a point, to prepare it for the roof attachment.*

lengths of grapevine, consider that you may need to wire the screening in place. Trim the excess screening and lay sheet moss over the entire inside of the wreath.

Cut the stems of the millet 5" to 6" (12.7cm to 15.2cm) in length. Insert the stems all around the outside edge of the wreath. If necessary, glue in place to hold. Using the large needle, string the peanuts tightly on the fishing line. Loop and drape the line over the edge of the wreath. Attach at several spots with the fishing line.

### FORMING BIRDSEED BALLS:

Mix all the ingredients together in a large bowl. Refrigerate for several hours, then form into balls. Cut a rectangle of chicken wire and shape it around each of the balls. Fit the wire snugly around the balls. If you wish, roll the ball back in birdseed. Use short lengths of wire to attach the balls to the wreath. Be sure to bury the ends of all the wires so that the birds do not receive pokes as they are eating.

### BUILDING MINI BIRDHOUSES:

Cut a 3" (7.6cm) long piece of the 1-1/2" (3.8cm) diameter birch branch. Leave one end flat and on the opposite end form a point. Drill a 3/4" (1.9cm) hole in the front of the branch. Drill a 1/4" (.6cm) hole

under the 3/4" (1.9cm) hole. Glue a 3/4" (1.9cm) long x 1/4" (.6cm) wide dowel rod into the 1/4" (.6cm) hole for a perch.

Cut one 1/4" (.6cm) thick board 2-1/4" (5.7cm) x 2-1/4" (5.7cm). Cut a second board 2-1/4" (5.7cm) x 2" (5.1cm). Glue these together at the pointed end to form the roof of the birdhouse. Use a few finishing nails per roof for extra security. Repeat to form two more birdhouses.

Drill a 1/4" (.6cm) hole in the bottom of each of the birdhouses. Cut three pieces of dowel rod different lengths and glue one into the bottom of each birdhouse. Glue these three into the top of the wreath near the back of the grouping.

Fill the center of the wreath with birdseed. Hang the wreath and prepare to enjoy the visits of many feathered friends. Change the mixture of the seed to attract different types of birds.

### GREAT IDEA!

String peanuts in long rows and hang like garland in your trees. Peanuts are especially attractive food for bluebirds, jays, mockingbirds, sparrows, and woodpeckers.

# BUTTERFLY GARDEN FOUNTAIN

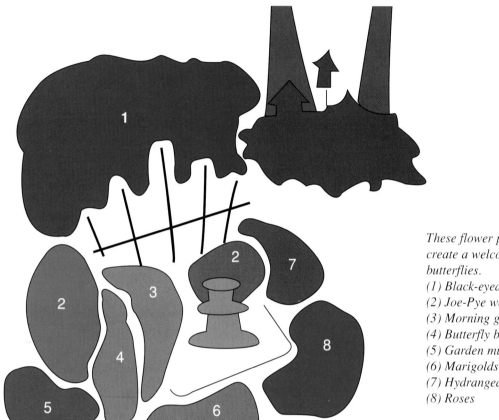

These flower placements create a welcome haven for butterflies.
(1) Black-eyed Susans
(2) Joe-Pye weed
(3) Morning glory
(4) Butterfly bush
(5) Garden mums
(6) Marigolds
(7) Hydrangea
(8) Roses

After a rain, butterflies often congregate around puddles. Birdbaths and gently flowing fountains are also favorite spots to gather. This fountain is easy to create and regulate using a small submersible pump with a flow-rate adjuster.

## COLLECTING SUPPLIES:

One 5" (12.7cm) clay saucer
One 9" (22.9cm) clay saucer
One 3-1/4" (8.2cm) clay pot
One 5" (12.7cm) clay pot
One small submersible pump with a
   flow-rate adjuster (150 volt 60HZ)
5" (12.7cm) length 3/8" (.9cm) plastic
   tubing
Drill and 3/8" (.9cm) drill bit
Small round bastard file
Silicone glue
Gravel

## BUILDING THE FOUNTAIN:

The water pump and tubing for the butterfly garden fountain are hidden inside the construction of clay pots and saucers.

3¼″ clay pot
5″ clay saucer
5″ clay pot
9″ clay saucer

Mark the center of the 5" (12.7cm) clay saucer. Soak in water for at least one hour before drilling. At the marking, drill a hole large enough to snugly fit the plastic tubing.

*Be sure to soak the saucer in water for at least one hour before drilling the hole.*

File four equally spaced notches around the upper edge of the 5" (12.7cm) pot. These are to facilitate the recycling of the water. One of the notches will be for the pump's electrical cord.

*Use a small round bastard file to create four notches along the edge of the large clay pot.*

Glue the bottom of the 5" (12.7cm) saucer to the bottom of the 5" (12.7cm) pot. Glue the bottom of the 3-1/4" (8.2cm) clay pot in the top of the 5" (12.7cm) saucer.

Insert the tubing in the 5" (12.7cm) clay pot and feed it up through to the smaller pot. It should extend less than halfway into the small pot.

Using the suction cup on the bottom of the pump, secure it to the center of the 9" (22.9cm) saucer. Place the tower of the two pots and smaller saucer over the pump, attaching the tubing to the pump.

Place gravel in the smaller pot to cover the tubing. Be sure the gravel is large enough not to fall into the tubing or it may clog the flow of water.

**Special Note: When using the fountain outdoors, always connect the pump to a ground-fault circuit interrupter.**

When creating a haven for butterflies, plan the placement of the flowers and fountains. Butterflies need to feel secure and search out protected areas. The small trellis placed behind the water fountain provides a bit of security while they are drinking from the fountain.

To change the location of your butterfly garden, place selected plants in containers and move as desired. Adjust the water flow so it is gently cascading over the sides.

The pump is being used to keep the water moving slowly.

## GREAT IDEA!

Butterflies also like to dine at a fruit bar. Place an old plastic dinner plate on a fence post, rock or crate in the garden. Keep it about waist high so you can easily observe the butterflies.

Cut overripe pears in half and add chunks of cantaloupe and watermelon. It may take a few days, but eventually butterflies will dive into the fruit bar. Do not worry if the fruit is rotting as it is most attractive to the butterflies in this state.

Butterflies eat by sucking liquids up through their proboscis, so the more rotten the fruit, the easier it is to suck. If you observe closely, you can even watch them use their straw-like proboscis.

# TREASURED BIRDHOUSES

When my sons were young, they used to love to visit with their grandfather for the day. One year, after one of these visits, they came home with birdhouses that they built (with Grandpa's help). The houses were a bit lopsided yet certainly prized treasures. The boys held them tightly in their arms and proudly displayed their creations.

They wanted to paint the houses, anticipating that a bird family would select these for their homes. My husband took the boys in the basement and allowed them to select whatever color they thought was appropriate for their new visitors. As they looked over the many colors on the shelf, the boys thought long and hard. Joey selected bright blue and Jimmy thought that bright orange was best for his house! My husband tried to explain that perhaps brown, soft green, or beige might make the houses appeal to birds in search of a natural environment. The boys insisted on their bright colors, explaining that they wanted to be sure the birds "saw" the houses.

So it was — bright blue and orange. My husband and I chuckled as the boys painted. We were sure no self-respecting bird would go near these houses. Frankly, we were a bit concerned that the boys would be upset when no birds selected their home.

Together, we went out in our yard to hang the houses on the "perfect" trees. They were easy to view from our kitchen window. Trust me, we could SEE those houses from our kitchen window!

We watched sporadically for a few days, waiting for birds to select these sites. The boys were SURE they would arrive. As the days passed, no birds claimed the houses as a residence.

In hopes of relieving their disappointment, I started to prepare a story to tell the boys. Fortunately I never had to tell the story. One morning Joey called out, "A bird! A bird has moved into my house!" As we watched closely, there indeed was a bird flying in and out of the house with small bits of nesting materials. The next thing we knew, another family had moved into Jimmy's house!

We watched all summer. The bird families came and went and eventually grew strong enough to leave.

The next spring another family claimed residence. This continued for several years. Eventually, the houses literally fell apart as they hung in the tree. The birdhouses didn't last forever, but the memories will always remain!

# BIRDHOUSE TABLE DESIGN

**B**ring in the beauty of the outdoors and display this birdhouse design in a quiet, sunlit area of your home.

## COLLECTING SUPPLIES:

*One wooden birdhouse, 9"
     (22.9cm) high x 5" (12.7cm)
     wide x 6" (15.2cm) long
Approximately thirty 1/4" (.6cm)
     diameter birch branches, cut
     15" to 18" (38.1cm to 45.7cm)
     long
6-8 sweet huck branches, cut 18"
     to 24" (45.7cm to 61cm) long
8-10 stems dried red amaranthus
12-15 stems orientalis
One 6" (15.2cm) clay pot broken
     into small pieces
Two 2" (5.1cm) clay pots
One 2" (5.1cm) feathered bird
Two 4-1/2" (11.4cm) feathered birds
8" x 12" (20.3cm x 30.5cm) piece of
     cardboard
Wood tone floral spray
Basil colored floral spray
Spanish moss
Small block dry floral foam
Glue
Pruners
"U" shaped floral pins*

These natural designs enhance the beauty of wood paneling and the antique table.

## CREATING THE DESIGN:

Spray the cardboard with wood tone floral spray to match the birch branches. Glue the birch branches closely together on top of the cardboard to form a flat base for the birdhouse. Don't worry if the branches aren't even, just arrange them naturally.

Spray the birdhouse with the basil floral spray and attach the birdhouse to the birch branch base. Glue the Spanish moss in a thin layer and completely cover the roof. Glue small pieces of the broken clay pot on top of the Spanish moss, then glue a small block of floral foam behind the birdhouse.

Cover the block with Spanish moss and secure with floral pins. To form a natural grouping, insert a few sweet huck branches and several stems of orientalis and red amaranthus.

Embellish the front of the birdhouse with smaller clay pots, Spanish moss, and small pieces of dried materials. Attach the three birds to add a welcoming touch to the design.

# BIRDHOUSE WREATH

Nature lovers will find this design appealing with its use of natural materials and birds. Use it in a grouping with the Birdhouse Table Design to create an outdoor feeling in a casual living or family activity area.

## COLLECTING SUPPLIES:

### FOR THE WREATH:

*One 18" (45.7cm) grapevine wreath*
*6-8 sweet huck branches, cut 12" to 24"*
   *(30.5cm to 61cm) long*
*Several stems of dried red amaranthus,*
   *orientalis, nigella, and safflower, cut 4"*
   *to 6" (10.2cm to 15.2cm) long*
*3 dried sunflower heads*
*Three 3" (7.6cm) mushroom style birds*
*Two 2-1/2" (6.4cm) feathered robins*
*One 4" (10.2cm) red cardinal*
*Sheet moss*
*Glue*

### FOR MINI BIRDHOUSES:

*8" (20.3cm) long x 2" (5.1cm) diameter*
   *birch branch*
*4" (10.2cm) long x 1/4" (.6cm) diameter*
   *dowel rod*
*13" (33cm) long x 1-1/8" (2.8cm)*
   *wide x 1/4" (.6cm) thick*
   *plywood board*
*Wood glue*
*Small hand saw*
*Drill with 3/4" (1.9cm) bit and 1/4"*
   *(.6cm) bit*
*Small finishing nails*
*Hammer*

## BUILDING THE MINI BIRDHOUSES:

Cut a 4" (10.2cm) long piece of the 2" (5.1cm) diameter birch branch. Cut the branch in half lengthwise so that the front is round and the back is flat. Leave one end flat and form a point at the opposite end of each. Drill a 3/4" (1.9cm) hole in the front of the branch on the rounded side. Drill a 1/4" (.6cm) hole under the 3/4" (1.9cm) hole. Glue a 1" (2.5cm) long x 1/4" (.6cm) wide dowel rod into the 1/4" (.6cm) hole for a perch.

Cut one 1/4" (.6cm) thick board 3-1/4" (8.2cm) x 1-1/8" (2.8cm). Cut a second board 3" x 1-1/8" (7.6 x 2.8cm). To form the roof of the birdhouse, glue these together at the pointed end. For extra security use a few finishing nails per roof. Repeat to form three additional birdhouses.

## CREATING THE DESIGN:

In the center of the wreath, attach the sweet huck branches in a vertical fashion. Glue the mini birdhouses to the wreath as shown. At the base of the wreath, create a crescent design with the red amaranthus. Add the sunflower heads. Fill in with stems of orientalis, nigella, and safflower. Glue the birds in place as desired.

*Red amaranthus, sunflowers, orientalis, nigella, and safflower are arranged naturally at the base of this design.*

# PEANUT BUTTER PINE CONE AND BIRDSEED WREATH

*This elegant stone and wrought iron fence is a perfect location for the Peanut Butter Pine Cone and Birdseed Wreath.*

Threé wonderful use of texture and color in this wreath make it a feast for the eyes! It will attract many types of birds. The squirrels will love it too! The day we photographed this wreath, a friendly squirrel stayed off to the side and intently watched us. I thought the wreath was safe on this beautiful entranceway gate, so I went into the garden to continue photography. Later, when I returned, I found our friendly squirrel perched right on top of the wreath! He was eating to his heart's content. He looked at me as if to say, "Just try to get me down!" Fortunately, we had already taken the photos!

*Raffia adds a natural touch and added texture to this wreath that birds of all types will love!*

## COLLECTING SUPPLIES:

*One 18" (45.7cm) straw wreath*
*Three oranges*
*Approximately 50 pine cones of assorted sizes and varieties*
*Peanut butter*
*Birdseed*
*2 oz. bunch dried safflower*
*3 yards (2.74m) of 1-3/4" (4.4cm) wide green wired mesh ribbon*
*3 yards (2.74m) of 2" (5.1cm) wide terra cotta stretch mesh ribbon*
*Raffia*
*"U" shaped floral pins*
*Glue*
*Cloth covered wire or chenille stem to secure bow*

## CREATING THE DESIGN:

Use the two types of ribbon to form a layered bow with long streamers. Attach to the center top of the wreath.

Cut the oranges in half and scoop out the insides. Allow a day for them to air dry. With glue and floral pins, attach the halves to the wreath at various places. Be sure all the cups of the oranges face upward.

Cover approximately twelve to sixteen of the larger pine cones with peanut butter. Roll in birdseed that has been placed on a flat paper plate. Leave one side of the pine cone without peanut butter or birdseed to allow you to easily glue the cones to the wreath. Glue these cones equally spaced around the wreath. Fill in around the bow and seed covered cones with plain pine cones.

Break off clusters of safflower and glue them around the wreath between the cones. Loop and drape the streamers of the bow around the wreath, then weave lengths of raffia between the pine cones and flowers.

After hanging the wreath, fill the orange cups with birdseed. Add more birdseed as necessary. You can also rejuvenate the peanut butter pine cones by spreading more peanut butter on them and pressing more birdseed into the peanut butter.

*Spread peanut butter on the pine cones.*

*After cutting the orange in half, scoop out the insides, leaving as much skin as possible.*

*Roll the pine cones in birdseed. Be sure to leave one side without peanut butter and birdseed, and glue that side to the wreath.*

*Use a floral pin and glue to attach the orange cups to the wreath after they have dried for at least one day.*

## GREAT IDEA!

Make four equally spaced holes around the top edge of the dried orange cup and tie on raffia as a hanger. Fill the cup with birdseed and hang from evergreen trees for the holidays.

# BUTTERFLY GARDEN CHAIR

I found this chair when visiting a local flea market. The wicker seat was broken. This was fine, because I really wanted a touch of nostalgia, which was provided by the nearly antique chair frame. After cleaning the chair, it took on a whole new life as the base for a planted butterfly and ivy garden. Throughout the day, I especially love watching the design change. As the sun moves in the sky, the shadows play and dance across the chair. You can even add color to the design by first painting the chair, then creating the garden.

## COLLECTING SUPPLIES:

*Chair with wicker seat removed*
*Soft mesh screening*
*Sheet moss*
*Potting soil*
*Staple gun*

## PLANTS:

*English ivy*
*Marigolds*
*Stella d' Oro lilies*
*Strawberry parfait dianthus*
*Red Crown Jewel garden mums*
*Sunny Border Blue*
*Joe-Pye weed*
*Miniature roses*

## CREATING THE DESIGN:

Remove the seat from the chair. Remove any residue such as nails or tape. Clean the chair thoroughly. Paint if desired. Staple the screening into the seat area. To hold moss and potting soil, be sure to allow the screening to sag severely in the middle.

Line the screening with a layer of sheet moss, then fill with potting soil and add plants. Weave the vines around the back and legs of the chair. This will enhance the natural look of the chair, making it seem part of the plants. To cover the stapled screening and hold moisture, add extra moss around the edges of the plants.

*Left: A flea market find turns into a wonderful garden chair to attract butterflies in your garden.*

*Staple the screening along the edges of the chair seat. You can add a fresh coat of paint to the chair to give it a face-lift.*

*Place a layer of moss at the bottom of the screening before adding the soil to act as drainage for the plants.*

# NATURAL FEATHER SWAG

*This striking swag blends beautifully with its surroundings and creates a visual bridge between indoors and outdoors.*

A re you looking for something striking to add to a den, family room, or recreation area? Try this design. The dramatic look of pheasant feathers adds an appealing accent to this swag created with a plethora of natural materials. With lengths of raffia in their beaks, the birds appear as if they are preparing a nest.

## COLLECTING SUPPLIES:

*One 20" (50.8cm) straw swag*
*1 lb. green baby eucalyptus*
*One 2 oz. package German statice*
*One 2 oz. package preserved ming fern*
*Five 15" to 18" (38.1cm to 45.7cm) long*
*    golden pheasant tails*
*Four 15" to 18" (38.1cm to 45.7cm) long*
*    zebra pheasant tails*
*One 2 oz. package natural raffia*
*Three 5" (12.7cm) long feathered birds*
*Ten assorted pods: lotus pods, okra pods,*
*    protea flats, and bell cups*
*One natural branch approximately 30"*
*    (76.2cm) long*
*"U" shaped floral pins*
*Glue*

## CREATING THE DESIGN:

Cut the eucalyptus and ming fern into 5" to 7" (12.7cm to 17.8cm) long pieces. Cut the statice into 3" to 4" (7.6cm to 10.2cm) long pieces. Form a cluster with one ming fern, one statice, and three eucalyptus stems.

*Cluster together eucalyptus, statice, and ming fern to cover the form.*

Starting at one end of the swag, use a floral pin to position the clusters facing out, overlapping each other. Work toward the center of the swag. Leave a 4" (10.2cm) opening at the center for the pod cluster. Repeat, working from the other end of the swag.

Position the feathers diagonally, bisecting the curve of the swag. Use floral pins and glue to hold in place.

Pin and glue the branch across the diagonal line of feathers. Cut the stems of the pods to 2" (5.1cm) length and glue the pods in a cluster at the center of the swag. Glue the birds along the branch. Loop and drape lengths of raffia throughout the design.

*Start at the end of the swag and attach clusters with floral pins. Each new row will cover over the ends of the former row.*

# TIPS

✤ Drill holes in a log and fill with seed or suet to use as a bird feeder. Hang vertically from leather straps or thin waterproof cording.

✤ To add realism, use artificial feathered birds and purchased nests with natural looking wreaths or baskets. Position the birds to suggest animation. String ribbon or raffia lengths from the birds' beaks to hint at nest building activities.

✤ Create a whimsical birdhouse by turning a clay pot upside-down, painting it a light color, and gluing assorted pressed flowers around it. Use a clear acrylic finish to protect the flowers. Add cut sticks for doors and windows. Use thinly sliced bark to fashion into a roof.

✤ To attract birds during the holidays, create a garland of birdseed covered foam balls and dried fruit slices. Thread small foam balls covered with peanut butter and then rolled in birdseed on lengths of raffia. For an outdoor winter bird treat, alternate with dried orange, apple, or lemon slices.

✤ For a design that would blend with almost any decor, use tall pheasant feathers in a basket or in a natural container. For added interest, attach small pods and cones to long wires and insert them between the feathers.

✤ For an unusual wreath design, glue short pheasant feathers or peacock eyes to a cardboard ring.

✤ To feed the birds during the holiday season, decorate your outdoor trees with strings of popcorn, cereal, or cranberries.

# PART THREE
## Nature

The beauty of nature has always had an invigorating influence on me. When I was younger, I would often ride my bike out into the metro parks system. I hiked through trails and along stream beds and became lost for hours. I loved looking for unusual rocks and tried very hard to skip stones across the water. I would lie on my stomach and study the plants and flowers in detail, as well as the ground with its multitude of insects.

On the subject of looking for details in nature, here is a challenge for you. Somewhere on these two pages is a small toad that we found when we were shooting the photography for this chapter. He rested just long enough for us to get his picture before he hopped off into the woods. Look around. Can you find him? While you are looking for the toad, examine the beauty and intricacy of nature in all the items we found that day.

This excercise reminds me of the book, *Where's Waldo*. My son Jim and I used to cuddle in one or the other's bed each evening. We slowly worked our way through the book, looking for Waldo and other hidden items on each page. This ritual strengthened our ability to visualize small details. Additionally, this exercise strengthened the bond of mother and son as, together, we did this activity.

As a family, we would take this exercise one step further. We laid on our stomachs in the woods, and played games of "I Spy." When one of us spotted something, the others guessed what it was with the use of color or shape clues. Sometimes we simply looked at the objects around us, sharing our discoveries. As we hurry through our lives, the daily amount of detail that we miss is amazing.

On nature hikes, my sons found stones and tried to skip them multiple times across the water. They would also carefully examine the plants, flowers, and insects. The activities of the boys caused me to think back to my youthful days. It certainly seemed as if life had come full circle!

Try these activities with your family. Take the time to examine nature up close and personal. Then bring home some of the treasures you find and create special designs or projects for display. Candles, table centerpieces, wreaths, topiaries, photo frames, and birdhouses are just a few ways to use materials that have been gathered on a hike or a collecting excursion.

Whether you experience nature alone or with family members, the time spent is precious and creates more lasting memories.

# FINDING AND PREPARING ITEMS FROM NATURE

There are many places to find the treasures of nature. Be careful and do not remove any materials from public areas, state or national parks. In some places, it is against the law. Follow the rule that I have often seen posted in public areas — "Take with you only memories and leave behind only footsteps."

It is illegal in many states to pick plant material along the side of a state highway. This is also a dangerous practice. Ask permission of farmers or other land owners. Most guidebooks will mention if a plant is protected or if it is considered permissable to pick a weed. Your local garden club may also be able to provide you with a list of protected plants in your area. Do not pick a plant if you see only a few in the area. When in doubt, do not touch.

When it's appropriate to gather, take along a field guide of natural materials. Purchase a guide that includes a wide range of elements in addition to flowers. Dress to protect your legs and arms. Gloves, insect repellent, and sunscreen are a good idea.

When gathering pods, wait until the seeds are ripe. To ensure a new crop next year, scatter the seeds in the growing area.

Collect pine cones after they fall from the tree. Place them in a warm area and allow them to open. The cones will darken, deteriorate, and become soft and unattractive if they are on the ground too long.

Wash all cones in water. Use a stiff wire brush to remove debris. To remove the pitch from fresh cones and add a shine, place them on an old pan or cookie sheet. Bake cones at 200 degrees F until the pitch melts. Note: If you bake them too long, the cones will turn dark.

The odor of cones baking is unpleasant.

Be sure to do this on a day when you can have the windows or doors open for ventilation. Since the baking pans will become discolored from the baking process, use only old pans that are no longer being used for food.

Baking the pine cones will also ensure the elimination of small bugs or insects that are living inside. Many projects or pieces of furniture have been ruined by bugs found in the cones.

Gather nuts and pods in late summer and early fall. Remove soil with a brush and hang the pods in a dry, well-ventilated area. To kill all insects, bake the nuts and pods on an old cookie sheet for 20 to 30 minutes in a 200 degree F oven.

To discourage mice and other rodents, after the nuts have cooled, store them in metal cans with mothballs. Purchased nuts do not need to be prepared in this manner.

When gathering plants, never pull them out by their roots. Cut the stems cleanly and process quickly after cutting. If immediate attention is not possible, place the stems in water until you are ready to use. Collect gatherings on a dry day. Bring along some type of box, basket or bucket to hold the treasures on the way home.

Avoid poison oak, ivy, and sumac. Know how to identify them.

If you collect mosses or lichens, spray them with an insecticide. This eliminates any infestation of insects in your home or furniture.

# NATURE INSPIRED GRAPEVINE WREATH

*This wreath design must be oversized and dramatic to command attention in this beautifully natural setting.*

I designed this wreath for the front door of my friend's home. They permitted us to use their beautiful house for all projects in this chapter and others shown individually throughout this book. View these photographs and enjoy their home with me. Their home in Ohio, located in the woods, is away from the main road. Interestingly, from this road the house is not even visible. It is only after driving in the front entrance and through a small wooded area that you get the first view of this fabulous front door. This house has been intentionally designed to coexist with nature.

It was important to consider the house and its setting when designing the wreath.

Since the house is very large, the wreath needed to be oversized and dramatic. Nothing small or modest would do in this case. The materials selected were also large and dramatic. For visual appeal, I utilized a variety of textures.

The color selection was also critical to

the success of the design. All the colors were natural, yet I took care to select colors across a broad "natural" spectrum.

The various color tones allow for better viewing of each pod, flower, or leaf. Each leaf stands out against the rest, yet all blend together and create a striking design.

## COLLECTING SUPPLIES:

*One 24" (61cm) grapevine wreath*
*(1) 6 stems each golden yellow*
*    and basil green preserved hops — cut*
*    12" (30.5cm) long*
*(2) 5 stems yellow dried yarrow*
*(3) 30 stems dried poppy pods*
*(4) 3 dried papyrus heads*
*(5) 4 dried neri pods*
*(6) 3 dried sea grape leaves*
*(7) 3 sponge mushrooms*
*(8) 3 bronze palms*
*(9) 4 mahogany pods*
*(10) 2 stems esperance nut*
*(11) 5 stems dried celosia*
*(12) 5 stems preserved Queen Anne's lace*
*A small amount of each: black lichen,*
*    sheet and reindeer mosses*
*Glue*

*Clusters of striking materials create a beautiful, abundant look. Extend the materials away from the wreath to add depth to the design.*

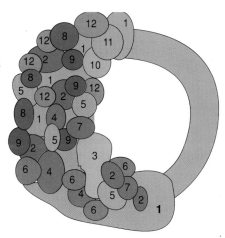

*The naturals and drieds are placed in clusters around the design, with a layer of hops under the flowers.*

## CREATING THE DESIGN:

Over 2/3 of the left side of the wreath, glue a covering of hops in a crescent shape. Allow the hops to droop and extend away from the wreath form.

Add 5" (12.7cm) long clusters of yarrow, spaced equally between the hops.

Provide a great deal of depth in the design by inserting the remainder of the focal flowers. Achieve this by allowing the materials to extend away from the wreath and toward the viewer. Be careful not to "stuff" all the materials together. Rather, allow each its own space, thereby creating visual depth.

Glue a large cluster of poppy pods to the lower 1/3 of the design. Allow the pods to extend 6" to 8" (15.2cm to 20.3cm) away from the wreath. Add two papyrus heads, two neri pods, three sea grape leaves, and three sponge mushrooms around the poppy pods. Cut larger items slightly shorter than the poppy pods and insert deeper in the design.

Insert a line of 5" (12.7cm) long bronze palm in the outside edge of the upper line of the design. Place 5"(12.7cm) long mahogany pods between the bronze palms. Insert two neri pods and one papyrus head just above the focal area.

Cut the esperance nut stems into 8" (20.3cm) long sections and insert randomly throughout the design. Add celosia stems in the upper end of the crescent. Add five 7" (17.8cm) long stems of Queen Anne's lace to the top 1/3 of the design. Allow the stems to extend several inches from the wreath.

# TAPESTRY BOX

My son Joe and I have had the opportunity to take several trips together. We have taped numerous television shows on the West Coast. When he competed in the National High School Speech Competition in North Carolina, we had the opportunity to explore East Coast nature. On one weekend excursion, we visited Fallingwater, an incredible home that intentionally coexists with nature and the geography of the area. Designed by Frank Lloyd Wright, the home even includes boulders and a waterfall!

During each of these trips, I found bits of nature — a rock, a pine cone, a seashell, etc.

When Joe graduated from high school and was about to begin his journey to college, I decorated the lid of a box with the collected treasures. I did not put anything inside the box. I told him that it was filled only with the memories of our trips. If he needs a bit of strength, a break from a hectic day, or a reminder of a hug, I suggested he open the box to relive the memories. He loved this special gift and reports that he often uses his memory box and enjoys the reflective times.

Use this idea as inspiration to create your personal collection of special materials. Choose a long low container and fill it with the natural materials you love. Weave a design of color and excitement using a variety of dried materials. Let the rich colors of a tapestry be your inspiration.

## COLLECTING SUPPLIES:

*One 20" (50.8cm) long by 10" (25.4cm) wide by 3" (7.6cm) deep natural oak tray*
*Sheet moss*
*4 stems large yellow dried yarrow — cut stems 3" (7.6cm) long*
*8 dried nigella heads*
*10 miniature dried pomegranates*
*8 dried globe thistles — cut 3" (7.6cm) long*
*4 mauve dried rose heads*
*12 stems mauve dried pepper berries — cut 3" (7.6cm) long*
*6 stems preserved bittersweet — cut 3" (7.6cm) long*
*4 cinnamon sticks — cut 4" (10.2cm) long*
*20 cinnamon sticks — cut 2-1/2" (6.4cm) to 3-1/2" (8.9cm) long*
*12 dried sarracenia stems — cut 10" (25.4cm) long*
*4 stems dried blue larkspur — cut 4" (10.2cm) long*
*Two sponge mushrooms*
*One sponge flower*
*Glue*

## CREATING THE DESIGN;

Line the inside of the tray with sheet moss and glue in place. Glue the stems of the sarracenia diagonally across the center of the tray. Allow some of the heads to extend in both directions. Use this as a dividing line.

On one side of the design, position clusters of yarrow, pomegranates, nigella heads, pepper berries, sponge mushrooms, and a mushroom flower in close groupings.

On the opposite side, position clusters of globe thistles, larkspur, rose heads, bittersweet, pepper berries, and cinnamon sticks. Cluster the cinnamon sticks in flat and standing positions.

*The Tapestry Box is a collection of beautiful, colorful, and textural materials.*

# SWEET GUM BALL AND TEASEL CANDLE RING

Candle ring designs need not be boring. To add a unique feature to this table design, try a new approach by using beeswax candles and miniature clay pots. Create with groupings of natural materials and attach to a grapevine wreath.

## COLLECTING SUPPLIES:

*One 12" (30.5cm) grapevine wreath*
*Approximately 30 dried teasels*
*Approximately 40 dried sweet gum balls*
*Approximately 15 dried nigella heads*
*Approximately 10 pear pods*
*Three 2-1/2" (6.4cm) clay pots*
*Sheet moss*
*Three 1" (2.5cm) square blocks of dry floral foam*
*Three 8" (20.3cm) beeswax candles*
*Glue*

*Beeswax candles are easy to make and enhance this candle ring design.*

## CREATING THE DESIGN:

Wire and glue two clay pots to the inside edge of the wreath. Wire and glue one pot to the top of the wreath between the other two pots. Glue the small foam blocks into the bottom of each of the clay pots.

Glue a cluster of teasels to the left side of the clay pot grouping. Glue a cluster of sweet gum balls behind the clay pots.

Glue a cluster of pear pods to the right side of the clay pot grouping.

Glue separate clusters of nigella heads, sweet gum balls, and teasels around the rest of the wreath. Leave a bit of space so the grapevine wreath is visible.

Tuck small amounts of sheet moss around the pots and clusters of naturals for a finishing touch.

# BEESWAX CANDLES

hese candles burn with a wonderful old-fashioned honey fragrance. Beeswax is naturally pliable when warm or at room temperature. If you are working with it in cold weather you may need to gently warm it with a hair dryer or heater, but be careful not to melt it!

If the wax looks frosty or dull, it has developed "bloom." This is a natural characteristic of beeswax. To restore the original color, simply warm the surface with a hair dryer, thereby removing the bloom.

## COLLECTING SUPPLIES:

*Three 8" (20.3cm) squares of beeswax for three 8" (20.3cm) candles*
*27" (68.6cm) of candle wicking*

## CREATING THE DESIGN:

Cut three wicks 9" (22.9cm) long. Crimp the wax very tightly around the wick and pinch evenly to seal the entire edge. Continue to roll evenly and tightly.

Seal the end by smoothing the seam with your thumb.

For short and wide candles, cut the square of beeswax smaller.

*SPECIAL NOTE:*
*Never leave burning candles unattended.*

*Roll the beeswax around the wicking and finish the end of the candle by stroking with the warmth of your hand.*

# COVERING CONTAINERS

**M**y workroom is full of used containers that look old and tired and are really in need of a "face-lift." It is easy to give an old container new life by covering it with natural looking materials. The container will also enhance the entire mood of a floral design. Some designs are not appealing when featured in a plain plastic or glass container. Create looks that are inspiring and unified by incorporating the elements of design when customizing a container for use.

# BIRCH BRANCH COVERED CONTAINER

## COLLECTING SUPPLIES:

*One 9" x 3" (22.9cm x 7.6cm) round plastic cylinder container*
*Spanish moss*
*Natural raffia*
*25-30 birch branches cut 9" (22.9cm) long*
*Glue*
*To fill the container:*
 *3 large cattails*
 *50 setaria stems*
 *3 mushroom flowers*

## CREATING THE DESIGN:

Glue a light covering of moss all around the outside of the container.

Glue the branches over the moss covered container, approximately 1/2" (1.3cm) apart.

Use a double knot to tie several lengths of raffia around the top and bottom of the container. Trim away the excess.

The container is a simply arranged, loose grouping of three large cattails, approximately fifty stems of setaria, and three mushroom flowers. For a balanced apperance, the arrangement should extend at least 1-1/2 to 2 times the height of the container.

# STONE FINISHED JARS

## COLLECTING SUPPLIES:

*Old mason jars*
*Spray or brush-on stone finish paint*

## CREATING THE DESIGN:

Create an interesting effect by applying stone finish to the outside of a plastic, glass, or metal container. This is an intriguing way to create a container for displaying some of the treasures you find on your nature walks.

# MOSS COVERED CONTAINER

## COLLECTING SUPPLIES:

*One clear plastic vase, 7-1/2" (19.1cm) tall with a 3-1/2" (8.9cm) square opening*
*Sheet moss*
*Assorted dried materials — tansy, miniature pine cones and pods, star anise, and celosia*
*Glue*
*To fill the container:*
 *ti tree stems*
 *dried iris pods*

## CREATING THE DESIGN:

Glue sheet moss to cover the outside of the container. Break the tansy and celosia into 1" (2.5cm) long pieces. Starting at the inside edge of the container, glue a row of tansy around the opening. Add a row of pine cones and then celosia. Finish with another row of pine cones. Around the base of the container, randomly glue miniature pods, star anise, and pine cones.

Fill the container with stems of ti tree and dried iris pods casually arranged.

*Left: Revitalize old containers by covering them with dried materials and mosses.*

# CARVED ROCKS

*Candles made in branches can add elegance and mood to outdoor get-togethers. Carve your favorite words in a rock and share it with someone you love.*

Our family loves to walk along or canoe in streams or rivers. We examine the trees and rocks along the shores. We love to collect rocks in all shapes, sizes, and color tones. We have painted them to look like animals or people. We have glued them together, then decorated them for gifts or just for fun. Recently we started to go one step farther with our rock creations and have carved words or verses in them. They make wonderful gifts, paper weights, or reminders of the important key words in our lives. Try this fun project. It is one way to have your very own words literally "carved in stone."

## COLLECTING SUPPLIES:

*Assorted soft rocks*
*Dremel® MultiPro™ rotary tool*
*Silicon carbide grinding stone bit in various
    shapes, sizes, and widths*
*Safety goggles*
*Dust mask*

## CREATING THE DESIGN:

With a pencil, lightly sketch the words or design on the rock. When carving, always wear safety goggles or glasses.

*First trace your design in pencil, then carve the words.*

If you are allergic to dust, a dust mask is helpful. Masks are inexpensive and available at most hardware stores.

Set the Dremel® speed at the medium high to high setting. Carefully trace over your pencil line with the drill bit. The more pressure you apply and the longer the bit remains in one place, the deeper the outline. Softer rocks work best. Do the carving outdoors to eliminate carving dust filtering throughout the house.

Try carving names, inspirational thoughts, words, or design motifs such as flowers or leaves.

## GREAT IDEA!

Line your garden or other pathway with rocks carved with words. On each rock, write a different word in the statement. Periodically rearrange the words and create new sayings!

# BARK CANDLES

Candles set a mood and create an image. Picture candles flickering with candlelight on a coffee table, fireplace mantel, or holiday table. Use any type of wood. Birch branches are especially nice.

Planning an outdoor party? Use citronella candles to help ward off the bugs and create a visually exciting atmosphere. Place fresh or dried materials in clusters around the branches to add color and variety.

### COLLECTING SUPPLIES:

*Branches — at least 2-1/2" (6.4cm) diameter in whatever length you choose*
*Tea lights*
*Electric drill*
*1-1/2" (3.8cm) drill bit*

### CREATING THE DESIGN:

Drill holes wide enough and deep enough to fit tea lights. Trim away excess bark to prevent a fire hazard. Insert tea lights into the holes and change when needed.

*SPECIAL NOTE:*
*Never leave burning candles unattended.*

*An electric drill and wide bit create wells for candles to be inserted.*

# ARCHITECTURAL TOPIARIES

Clean, clear, basic lines and shapes in design relate an architectural feeling, inspiring the creation of dramatic effects. Create a dramatic grouping by using cone shapes covered with natural elements. Use pressed or preserved leaves of different textures to cover various shapes. Interesting bases add an appealing accent and help to blend with the setting.

## COLLECTING SUPPLIES:

*One each 9" (22.9cm), 12" (30.5cm), and
    15" (38.1cm) foam cones*
*Approximately 100 pressed small black
    walnut leaves for 15" (38.1cm) cone*
*Approximately 75 assorted pressed small
    black walnut, oak, elm, and burning
    bush leaves for 12" (30.5cm) cone*
*Approximately 50 pressed lamb's ear leaves
    for 9" (22.9cm) cone*
*9 natural birch branches, 1/4" (.6cm)
    diameter — cut 6" (15.2cm) long*
*Sheet moss*
*3 Roman lights — 3-1/2" (8.9cm) square by
    8-1/2" (21.6cm), 7-1/2" (19.1cm), and
    6-1/2" (16.5cm) high*
*Dry floral foam*
*Glue*

## CREATING THE DESIGN:

Create each of the cones in the same manner. Start at the top of the cone and, in a circular fashion, glue leaves in rows around the cone. Slightly overlap to completely cover. Design the cones with the same type of leaf or create with leaves of different colors and textures. When using several different leaves to cover a cone, alternate the leaf types as each row is added.

To form a trunk, insert three birch branches into the base of each cone. Glue a small block of dry floral foam into each of the Roman lights. Insert the ends of the birch branch trunks into the foam. Glue to hold in place. Lightly cover the foam with sheet moss.

*The topiary trunks are formed with multiple birch branches.*

## GREAT IDEA!

Use these topiaries in a grouping on a buffet table. Their shape is eye-catching and combines a visually intriguing mixture of textures and colors. Scatter additional leaves and natural materials around the base of the topiaries.

*Right: The clean, basic look of architecturally-inspired topiaries and natural balls creates a striking design element on a hearth.*

# PRESSED LEAF RING AND NATURAL BALLS

Use a variety of pressed and dried materials to cover foam shapes. Your imagination is the only limit when selecting varieties of natural materials useful for covering these shapes. Use the ring and balls in a grouping with the architectural topiaries to create a look of abundant simplicity.

## COLLECTING SUPPLIES:

*Three 4" (10.2cm) and two 5" (12.7cm) foam balls*
*Approximately 20 of each: small pressed oak, elm, black walnut, and burning bush leaves for 5" (12.7cm) ball*
*Approximately 25 pressed lamb's ear leaves for 4" (10.2cm) ball*
*Approximately 30 pressed black walnut leaves for 4" (10.2cm) ball*
*Spanish moss for 5" (12.7cm) ball*
*Approximately 100 star anise for 5" (12.7cm) ball*
*Approximately 40 rosehips for 5" (12.7cm) ball*
*Approximately 180 small dried rosebuds for 4" (10.2cm) ball*
*Approximately 180 tiny pine cones for 4" (10.2cm) ball*
*12" (30.5cm) foam ring with flat bottom*
*Approximately 50 burgundy pressed leaves*
*Sphagnum moss*
*Brown floral spray color*
*Rubber bands*
*Glue*

## CREATING THE DESIGNS:

To cover a ball shape with leaves, start at one point and glue the leaves in a row around the ball, overlapping slightly. Repeat with the remaining leaves, overlapping each row to completely cover the ball. When using several different leaves to cover a ball, simply alternate the types of leaves as you are creating each row.

Cover a foam ring with the same method. Use overlapping rows of pressed leaves and completely cover the ring. Add small tufts of moss for texture.

To cover a ball with tiny pine cones and rosebuds, spray the ball with a brown floral color. At one area on the ball, create a row that has one pine cone, one rosebud, etc., all the way around. Following that pattern, cover the entire ball in very tight rows.

After spraying brown, lightly cover one of the 5" (12.7cm) balls with Spanish moss and glue it in place. Starting at the top of the ball, glue the star anise spiraling all around the ball. Randomly glue the rosehips in the empty areas.

Create a twig ball by using smaller, softer stems to form the core. While the twigs are green and still flexible, soak in water and tightly wrap around the core. Continue until you reach the desired size ball. Hold together with rubber bands. Allow to dry to retain its shape.

*Glue the pressed leaves in rows on the foam ball.*

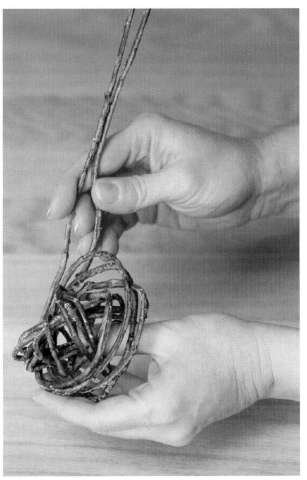

*Use green branches or soak narrow branches in water before shaping them into a ball form.*

## GREAT IDEA!

Use fragrant bay leaves to cover a foam ball. Hold in place with shiny gold studs or upholstery tacks. Also acceptable are eucalyptus leaves, rose petals, lavender, or spices. Display these decorated balls in a grouping by themselves, in a simple glass bowl, or nestled on a bed of preserved greenery.

# COVERED PICTURE FRAMES

*Spotlight your favorite memories with decorative picture frame embellishments.*

Memories are created daily. How exciting it is to capture some of these memories on film and be able to display them in an album or frame. The moss covered frame in this grouping holds one of those special memories for me. When my son Jim was young, I used to take him to a city park where there lived many, many ducks and geese. We would bring along old bread, crackers, or cereal and feed them whenever we had the opportunity. One day, I had purchased a new camera and decided to bring it along. That day the ducks and geese were especially frisky — so was Jimmy. He believed he was going to catch and hold one and began to chase them around the pond. As is imaginable, they were a lot faster than Jimmy. Their speed, however, did not dissuade him. I captured on film, his huge smile and the look of total delight on his face as he ran around and around. It was truly a memorable day for me so I wanted to display those memories for all to see. I created this frame with flowers from my garden, pressed around the same time I took the photograph. I get many compliments from friends and family about this picture and frame!

Create special frames and feature your favorite memory making photos.

# MOSS COVERED FRAME

## COLLECTING SUPPLIES:

One 7" x 9" (17.8cm x 22.9cm) wooden
frame with a 4" x 6" (10.2cm x
15.2cm) opening — the frame width
is 1-1/2"(3.8cm)
Sheet moss
Assorted pressed flowers and leaves —
lavender, heather, Queen Anne's
lace, daisies
Glue

## CREATING THE DESIGN:

Completely cover the frame with
moss. Glue a cluster of flowers at
the bottom right corner and at the
top left corner.

*Moss and pressed flowers create a striking frame to accent this
picture taken in the park.*

# WALLPAPER COVERED FRAME

## COLLECTING SUPPLIES:

One 11" x 12" (27.9cm x 30.5cm) wooden
frame with a 4-1/2" x 6-1/2" (11.4cm x
16.5cm) opening — the frame width is
3-1/4" (8.2cm)
13" x 12" (33cm x 30.5cm) wallpaper piece
in color of your choice — scraps from
an old wallpaper book can be used
Spray paint to coordinate with wallpaper
Pressed leaves — lamb's ear, dusty miller,
and burning bush leaves
X-acto™ knife
Spray adhesive

## CREATING THE DESIGN:

Spray the entire frame with a paint color
that coordinates with the wallpaper. Glue
the wallpaper to the frame with spray adhesive by spraying both the frame and the
back of the paper before placing the two
together. Use a knife to trim around the
picture opening and edges.

Glue the leaves in a pleasant grouping
around the bottom third of the frame.

*Use scraps of wallpaper and pressed leaves for a
warm outdoor look.*

*To get a clean edge, use a knife and cut along the
edge of the frame after the paper has been applied
to the wood.*

# LAVENDER COVERED FRAME

## COLLECTING THE SUPPLIES:

*One 10" (25.4cm) square wooden frame
with a 3" (7.6cm) square opening — the
frame width is 3-1/2" (8.9cm)*
*Spray paint to match lavender*
*Five 2 oz. bunches of dried lavender —
approximately 1000 stems*
*Twelve burdock burrs*
*28 gauge spool or paddle wire*
*Glue*

## CREATING THE DESIGN:

Spray the entire frame with paint that
will coordinate with the lavender stems.
Cut 120 stems, without flowers, 4"
(10.2cm) long. Use a short length of wire
to hold 30 stems together on both ends.
Repeat, forming a total of four bunches.
Glue one bunch on the frame at the middle
top of the opening. Repeat with the remaining bunches, equally spacing them around
the frame.

Cut the lavender into 3-1/4" (8.2cm) to
3-1/2" (8.9cm) long pieces. Form a bunch
with approximately 12 stems. Secure the
ends of the bunches with thin wire. Starting
at the outside edge, glue the bunches in an
arc-like fashion covering the frame. Work
to the inside, overlapping bunches to completely cover the frame. Around the opening of the frame, glue the burdock burrs
over the ends of the lavender bunches.

*Apply the lavender in small clusters, side-by-side,
to create a feeling of abundance.*

# TIPS

❖Beeswax candles are naturally tacky.
Gently press beads, sequins, shells, or other
lightweight items into the candle to create
your own original decorations. These candles make elegant gifts when tied in pairs
with raffia or festive ribbon.

❖Display dried materials in a glass
bowl by layering different types of items to
create a unique effect. Line a very deep
bowl or container with an unusual variety
of moss. Incorporate exciting elements such
as nuts in the shell, miniature cones and
pods, dried spices, seeds, and flower heads.

❖Shadow boxes work extremely well to
feature your natural collection of treasures.
Purchase or create a box with several small
compartments. Leave the back of the box

natural or use wallpaper or paint techniques
to add another dimension. Carefully select
items from nature that will fit each com-
partment. This idea can easily turn into a
"memory frame" by filling the compartments with items collected on excursions
with a particular friend or family member.
On a card, write your memories of each
item, then apply the card to the back of the
frame along with the current date.

❖Items from nature are especially wonderful when used to decorate for the fall
and winter holidays. You can add a bit of
sparkle or shine by spraying cones or pods
in metallic or glitter color tones and placing
these sprayed items intermixed with natural
items in bowls, baskets, or decorative
boxes.

*Grow lavender in your garden, then dry it and use it to create this aromatic framed design.*

# PART FOUR
# Garden

When I was growing up, my grandparents lived next door to me. I loved visiting and helping with the gardening. You would often see my grandmother in her cotton dress, apron, and big straw hat with a wicker gathering basket over her arm, digging and planting in the garden.

Every spare minute my father had, he would be working in his garden. Neither of our yards was very large, but both overflowed with roses, snapdragons, daisies, cucumbers, tomatoes, peaches, raspberries — and what seemed like every plant or flower available in the world!

What I remember most about my grandmother is her lilacs. She used to have a huge wall of them all along the back lot line of her yard. When they bloomed, they were a solid wall of color that obliterated every view of our neighbors. The view was breathtaking and the aroma was enticing. Each morning I would pick a lilac stem and carry it with me to school, taking small whiffs along the way. When I was older, I would place the stem above the visor of my car when I left each morning. At the end of the day, the flower still smelled wonderful even though its appearance looked a bit wilted. To this day, I think of my grandmother whenever I smell or see lilacs. What flower brings back special memories for you?

My father's treasures were his roses. He would prune and cultivate until they were the most magnificent in any nearby garden. I used to watch him as he cared for the roses, adding fertilizer and water. He used to place small pots of flowers, including miniature roses, all along the window ledge of the basement. All winter long, he would nurture and care for these flowers.

Perhaps it is these early memories that have made me so passionate about flowers. Flowers brighten the day, say "I love you" and "I'm sorry." Flowers help us celebrate, or soften the grieving process. It is no wonder so many people around the world love to garden.

Throughout history, the garden has been viewed as a central place in the spiritual quest for paradise. Our own personal gardens can be sanctuaries to bring refreshment, a place of growth, change, and peace. Unlike raw nature, designing a garden can reflect our personal taste, needs, and desires. Design a formal garden or create one that is casual. A garden is a place of self-expression, uniquely individual. It can be designed to labor in or relax in. It's your own private place. Timetables, calendars and the demands of others dominate our lives. The garden is a retreat . . . a private haven.

# CARING FOR CUT FLOWERS

Gather flowers from the garden early in the morning or late in the afternoon. Never gather flowers midday. During the middle of the day, the water content in the plant tissues is lowered by heat and sunlight. The reserves of sugar, which aid in the length of life for a flower, have not yet reached their maximum levels. Cut flowers with a sharp knife. Do not break or pull the stems or cut them with scissors, or you may damage the delicate tissues.

Always purchase fresh flowers from a reliable source. Buds and blossoms should not appear limp or soft. Select flowers with young, firm blossoms. Petals should

not be bruised. Look at the center — if pollen has built up, the flower will not last long after you get it home. Watch for mold forming under the flower head around the calyx. Look for buds at different stages of opening so they will not bloom all at once. Avoid roses with buds that are soft and mushy to the touch. Drooping foliage indicates older flowers that will not last long when brought home. Healthy looking foliage indicates healthy flowers. Check the stems for discoloration or sponginess.

Water is extremely important to cut flowers. It carries sugars and other nutrients that give support to the flower and the stem. The moment you bring flowers into the house, cut the stem ends again and put them in your deepest container of water with preservative solution. Several hours are necessary for store-bought, or overnight for garden flowers. The stems will absorb tepid or warm water more quickly than cold water. Place the container in a cool spot, free of drafts and let them take a good long drink. The water the flowers are in should be clear and clean. Murky container water and discolored, decaying stem ends indicate the presence of bacteria which will damage plant tissue and impede water absorption. Replace water often.

Keep your water buckets only for the use of flowers. Do not use them with other chemicals or solutions whose residue can be harmful.

The stem of a flower allows it to take in as much water as possible. If not kept in water, cut stem ends can dry out. Always re-cut the stems of foliage and flowers before placing them in water. It is most effective to cut the stems while they are underwater. Cut stem ends at an angle just before arranging to eliminate any air bubbles that formed while preparing. Air bubbles prevent water from flowing up the stem, thereby shortening the life of the flower.

Fresh cut flowers need nutrients to stay alive. While the flower is growing, sugars move up from the mother plant. The sugar-flow stops when a flower is cut. Preservative solutions provide the food that moves up the stem into the flower. Adding floral preservatives to the water will greatly increase the life of the flower, help retain the color longer, and may even enhance the fragrance. Follow the instructions on the preservative package to determine the ratio of unsoftened water that should be mixed with the preservative solution.

Remove all leaves from the flower stem that will be submerged below the water line. They will quickly decay and add stem-plugging bacteria into the water.

Fresh flowers are temperature sensitive. Keep them protected from temperature extremes. Each flower has a temperature gauge. If the temperature becomes too high, food is used up too fast. Water is then lost faster than it is replaced. Never place a fresh flower arrangement on top of the television set or in a sunny window. The heat may become too strong.

Dry air also affects fresh flowers. After a flower is cut, it perspires by losing water vapor from the surface of the leaves. Flowers lose water faster when the air is dry, causing them to wilt.

Do not put fruit and flowers in a refrig-erator together. Some fruits, especially apples, give off ethylene gas. Because flowers are sensitive to gases in the atmosphere, they may wilt, curl, or yellow if exposed.

Extend the life of a fresh floral design by properly saturating the fresh floral foam that will be used in preparation of the container. A block of fresh foam holds over 40 times its weight in water or about two quarts of water. Add more water daily.

If using fresh floral foam, place the stems firmly in the top and sides of the foam. Make sure that the ends remain in contact with the foam to ensure a continuous water supply. If you need to adjust the placement of a flower, remove the flower from the foam and reinsert it.

Condition stems in various ways before you place them in a vase, arrangement, or fresh floral foam. Different flower types require different conditioning methods, all having one common purpose — to enable them to take in as much water as possible. As a rule of thumb, cut all stems at an angle. Exceptions to this rule are woody stems like forsythia, lilac, and magnolia. Crush or split these stem ends. Gently hammer the tops or make a two inch vertical cut up the base of each stem with sharp shears or scrape the bark with a sharp knife several inches from the bottom.

Euphorbias, poppies, hollyhocks, and any flowers with a milky sap will last longer if you cauterize the end of the stem by holding it over a flame until it turns black. This prevents the sap from solidifying at the tip and blocking the intake of water.

Amaryllis, delphinium, and lupine have hollow stems. Up-end these, fill with water and plug with a piece of cotton. Hold your thumb over the end to prevent the cotton or water from escaping as you place each stem into the water-filled vase.

# DRYING FRUITS

Cut citrus fruits into 1/4" (.6cm) thick slices. Pat dry and place on a waxed paper covered cookie sheet. Bake in a very low oven (140 to 200 degrees F) for two to three hours, turning them several times. If the waxed paper starts to brown, replace it. Remove slices before they turn brown. Let them finish drying in a warm spot for a few more days.

Soak apple slices for fifteen minutes in a mixture of 1 quart of water, 1 tbs. Fruit Fresh, and 1 tbs. lemon juice before drying. Bake them in the same manner as the citrus slices.

You can also dry a whole lemon or a small orange. With a knife, make six to eight vertical slits into the rind. Stop before you reach the ends. Dry for several hours in the oven at 200 degrees F. Remove fruit before it begins to brown and let it continue to air dry slowly in a warm area. You may want to spray it with varnish or shellac to repel insects.

# GARDEN FOUNTAIN

**M**oving water is a wonderfully refreshing feature in a garden. It cools the air and delights the ear. For centuries, only the rich could enjoy this beauty. With the range of relatively inexpensive submersible pumps available, anyone can enjoy moving water in their garden. Waterfalls or fountains add healing sounds to the garden. They can be "tuned" through the careful arrangement of the height and angle of rocks or stones.

Introducing changes in the water pattern with rocks or ledges make the sounds produced seem as though they are at different levels of the scale. These sounds bring an added dimension of harmony to the garden.

*The Garden Fountain adds beauty and the sound of running water to a porch, deck, or garden.*

## COLLECTING SUPPLIES:

*One each 6" (15.2cm), 8" (20.3cm), 10" (25.4cm) and 18" (45.7cm) clay saucers*
*Two each 2-1/2" (6.4cm) clay pots*
*One 4-1/2" (11.4cm) clay pot*
*Two 6" (15.2cm) clay pots*
*One 10" (25.4cm) clay strawberry pot*
*Decorative rocks*
*Gravel*
*Potted plant for inside strawberry pot*

*One small submersible pump with a flow-rate adjuster (150 volt 60HZ)*
*Electric drill*
*3/8" (.9cm) drill bit*
*3/8" (.9cm) plastic tubing*
*Dremel® MultiPro™ rotary tool*
*Silicon carbide grinding stone bit*
*Small round bastard file*
*Silicone glue*

## CREATING THE DESIGN:

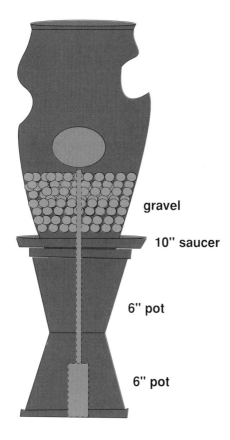

*The plastic tubing and pump extend up through the tallest clay pot tower of the fountain.*

File one notch in the upper edge of each of the saucers. Glue the 6" (15.2cm) saucer to the bottom of a 2-1/2" (6.4cm) pot. Place this grouping inside the 18" (45.7cm) saucer near the edge. Position the notch on the saucer to the left.

Glue the top of a 2-1/2" (6.4cm) pot to the bottom of the 4-1/2" (11.4cm) pot. Glue the 8" (20.3cm) saucer to the bottom of the 2-1/2" (6.4cm) pot. Place this tower to the right of the first pot and saucer positioned. Position the notch on the 8" (20.3cm) saucer so that the water will empty into the 6" (15.2cm) saucer.

File four equally spaced notches in the upper edge of one 6" (15.2cm) pot. One notch will be for the pump's electrical cord. Glue the bottom of the notched pot to the bottom of the other 6" (15.2cm) pot.

Mark the center on the bottom of the 10" (25.4cm) clay saucer. Soak in water for approximately an hour before drilling. At the marking, drill a hole large enough for the plastic tubing to fit snugly. Center and glue the saucer to the top of the un-notched 6" (15.2cm) pot. Center the hole in the bottom of the strawberry pot over the saucer and glue it to the saucer.

Insert the pump into the notched 6" (15.2cm) clay pot and feed the tubing up through to the strawberry pot. Place this tower behind the first saucer and pot positioned. Position the notch on the 10" (25.4cm) saucer so the water will empty into the 8" (20.3cm) saucer.

Before gluing all these down to the saucer, add water and see how well the saucers empty into each other. If necessary, reposition. Allow to dry and glue down the shorter two saucer/pot combinations. Do not glue the largest combination down so that you can get to the pump, if necessary.

You may need to adjust the flow of the water spouts. This is done with a wide sanding bit and a rotary tool as well as adjusting the flow directly from the pump.

Fill the inside of the strawberry pot with gravel up to the edge of the plastic tubing. Add decorative rocks in each of the saucers. Place a potted plant in the strawberry pot.

*SPECIAL NOTE:*
*Be sure to connect the pump to a ground-fault circuit interrupter when using it outdoors.*

## GREAT IDEA!

Make several garden fountains in different configurations and place them throughout your garden to add the beauty and sound of running water. To create a pedestal look, spray the fountain with a stone-finish paint and place on top of a bird bath base.

# LIVING WREATH

A fresh, growing wreath that lasts for years and years is a refreshing addition to any room in your home. Place daisies in water tubes. If you replenish the water, they will last for quite a while. Living wreaths can be made with several varieties of plants, such as succulents, flowering plants, and herbs. Follow the same instructions, just change the plant selection.

*The Living Wreath and Pot en Fleur design are strking when combined together in the corner of a room.*

## COLLECTING SUPPLIES:

Two 14" (35.6cm) wire wreath frames
Copper spool wire
Potting soil
2 large bags of sheet moss
Five 4" (10.2cm) potted ivy plants with long
    cascading ivy sections
2-1/2" (6.4cm) water tubes — filled with
    water
10 to 12 fresh white daisies

## CREATING THE DESIGN:

Wire the two wreaths together with copper wire to prevent rusting. Soak the moss thoroughly and drain it.

*Secure the two wire wreath forms together with copper wire.*

*Spread damp moss under the wreath form and fill the form with potting soil.*

Cover a large area with newspaper and plastic. Working on top of this, form a mat of sheet moss about 2-1/2 times the size of the wreath frame. Fill the inside of the frame with soil.

*Press the moss up and around the form, then completely wrap with copper wire.*

Pull the moss up and around the wreath frame, starting at the top, then the bottom, right side, and then left side. Wrap the wire around the wreath to secure the moss in place. Use scraps of moss to patch in empty areas and wrap with wire again to finish. This part is easiest with two people working together.

*Plant ivy in holes created with a pencil or stylus.*

Separate the ivy into single cuttings. Using a pencil or thin stylus, make a hole in the moss and gently insert the cutting. Cover the entire wreath in this manner, equally spacing the plants around the form. Use short lengths of copper wire bent into a "U" shape to secure trailing tendrils of ivy. As the wreath grows, you will need to continue to secure the tendrils to the wreath.

*Use "U" shaped pieces of copper wire to secure trailing ivy to the wreath form.*

Fill the florist water tubes with preservative treated water and insert a daisy in each. Position the daisies all around the wreath. Change the flowers as they begin to droop or with each season. Add water to the tubes daily.

I find that the best way to water this wreath is to take it down from the wall, place it in a deep sink or on a plastic covered countertop and water heavily. Allow to drain. If your metal frame is rusting, be sure not to get rust on your wall. Take another wire wreath form and wrap it in plastic. Hang it behind the moss form to provide separation between the wreath and the wall.

# POT EN FLEUR

Pot en Fleur is a French term for the art of combining fresh cut flowers with potted plants. Replenish cut flowers as needed; thus extending the life of the arrangement.

## COLLECTING SUPPLIES:

*One 12" (30.5cm) x 9" (22.9cm) x 2-1/2" (6.4cm) deep wicker tray basket*
*One 4" (10.2cm) African violet plant*
*One 4" (10.2cm) variegated needlepoint ivy plant*
*One 4" (10.2cm) dieffenbachia plant*
*5 stems fresh white larkspur — cut in lengths 10" to 18" (25.4 to 45.7cm) long*
*4 fresh pink roses — cut 4" to 8" (10.2cm to 20.3cm) long*
*4 stems fresh pink cushion mums — cut 4" to 6" (10.2cm to 15.2cm) long*
*3 clear plastic high drinking glasses, 3" to 4" (7.6cm to 10.2cm) high*
*1 block of fresh floral foam*
*Floral preservative*
*Sheet moss*
*Florists' foil*
*Potting soil*

## CREATING THE DESIGN:

Line the basket with florists' foil. Keep the plants in their pots and place them in the following positions in the basket: African violet, right front corner; ivy plant, left front corner; dieffenbachia, back left corner.

Place an empty clear plastic cup near the center back of the basket, one behind the African violet, and one between the violet and the ivy plants. Soak the floral foam in preservative-treated water. Cut a piece of foam to fit each cup and extend about one inch above the edge of the cup. Wedge the foam pieces into each of the cups.

Spread potting soil around the potted plants and cups. Remove the plants from their pots and replant them in their respective spots, filling in with potting soil as needed.

Insert the larkspur into the foam in the cup, positioned at the center back of the basket, forming a vertical cluster of flowers. Form a cluster with the roses, positioning them in the cup behind the African violet. Repeat with the cushion mums, placing them in the cup between the African violet and the ivy.

Remember that all of these are still living and water accordingly. To ensure long flower life, water fresh floral cups daily. Water and fertilize the green plants as you normally would. Add new flowers when the fresh flowers wilt. To eliminate contamination and to ensure the proper uptake of water, use new fresh floral foam with each new grouping of fresh flowers.

# GARDEN MOSS HAT

Long streamers of hanging amaranthus create a strking eye movement and balance the clustering of flowers at the crown.

A woodland sprite would be proud to wear this fashionable creation for any occasion. Use dried roses and other preserved garden materials to embellish a moss covered straw hat. The colors and textures are truly garden inspired.

## COLLECTING SUPPLIES:

One 14" (35.6cm) straw hat
Basil green floral spray color
Sheet moss
6 dried rose heads
5 clusters dried mauve pepper berries
Dried blue larkspur — cut in six 4" (10.2cm) lengths
Preserved foxtail foliage — cut in eight 4" (10.2cm) lengths
Sweet huck branches — cut in ten 4" (10.2cm) lengths
Preserved burgundy hanging amaranthus — cut in sixteen lengths 8" to 24" (20.3cm to 61cm)
Preserved ti tree — cut in 4" (10.2cm) lengths
Dried natural yarrow — cut in 3" (7.6cm) lengths
Six small dried daisy heads
Glue

## CREATING THE DESIGN:

Spray the hat inside and out with the basil floral color. Allow to dry. Cover the entire top of the hat with moss.

At the base of the hat crown, glue six roses in a cluster. Glue three clusters of yarrow into the center of the rose cluster. Glue small sprigs of larkspur, ti tree, and foxtail between the roses. Add short sweet huck branches for a finishing touch.

For a dramatic look, glue the hanging amaranthus in the center of the rose cluster so that it cascades down the back of the hat.

Equally space six clusters of yarrow around the brim of the hat. Glue the pepper berry clusters between the yarrow. Randomly glue the daisies and several larkspur florets between the yarrow and pepper berries.

## GREAT IDEA!

Freeze-dried flowers are becoming increasingly available across the country. Their fresh look remains for a long time and they are wonderful additions to this design. Check your local floral supplier and ask them about the availability of freeze-dried flowers.

*Right: The Pavé design and Garden Moss Hat are reminiscent of a French garden and coordinate beautifully with this French-inspired kitchen.*

# PAVE' DESIGN

Jewelers use the term pavé to describe the process of setting precious stones closely together so that no metal shows. This design captures that feeling while incorporating taller flowers, creating a terraced effect. Its combination of color and texture is reminiscent of a French garden.

## COLLECTING SUPPLIES:

*One 12" (30.5cm) diameter by 4" (10.2cm) deep wicker basket*
*Two full blocks fresh floral foam*
*Sheet moss*
*9 fresh purple liatris stems — cut 12" to 20" (30.5cm to 50.8cm) long*
*6 fresh pink snapdragon stems — cut 4" to 10" (10.2cm to 25.4cm) long*
*6 fresh white carnation heads — leave stems 2" (5.1cm) long*
*7 fresh pink roses — leave stems 2" (5.1cm) long*
*3 stems fresh yellow daisy pomps — cut 3" to 8" (7.6cm to 20.3cm) long*
*3 stems fresh white daisy pomps — cut 3" to 7" (7.6cm to 17.8cm) long*
*3 stems fresh small pink cushion mums — cut 3" to 6" (7.6cm to 15.2cm) long*
*Florists' foil*

## CREATING THE DESIGN:

Line the inside of the basket with florists' foil. Soak the floral foam as directed. Cut the blocks to fit and wedge, completely filling the basket. To continually add water, cut a wedge out of the back of the foam.

Dampen the sheet moss and apply a very light covering over the foam. Position the liatris in a vertical grouping near the back edge of the basket. Position the snapdragons to the right of the liatris grouping.

Insert the carnation heads along the front of the basket, following the curve of the basket. Insert the rose heads in the same manner, following the curve of the carnations.

Position the yellow daisy pomps to the left of the liatris grouping. Position the white daisies to the right of the snapdragons. The cushion mums are the shortest of the vertical groupings, positioned to the left of the yellow daisy pomps.

When inserting these flowers in each of their separate groupings, place the shorter flowers near the center of the liatris grouping. This allows the taller flowers to curve around the liatris, toward the back of the basket. The taller flowers "stair step" above the shorter flowers.

*Right: Rows and clusters of flowers make the Pavé design interesting to look at. The picture is completed with the antique French game table as a backdrop.*

# BABIES BREATH AND HEATHER TOPIARY

**F**loral topiary designs are frequently used for home decor accents — indoors or outdoors. This unusual design uses the beauty and delicacy of babies breath for the main form. It also allows a subtle backdrop to the cluster of flowers that explode from the top of the ball.

## COLLECTING SUPPLIES:

*Large bunch fresh babies breath — cut in 3" (7.6cm) lengths*

*24 stems of fresh heather — cut in 6" to 8" (15.2cm to 20.3cm) lengths*

*30 fresh yellow daisies — cut 3" (7.6cm) long*

*One 4" (10.2cm) pot of variegated needlepoint ivy*

*One block fresh floral foam, 3" (7.6cm) square (round off corners)*

*One block dry floral foam, 2-1/2" (6.4cm) square*

*One 12" (30.5cm) long x 1" (2.5cm) wide tree branch*

*Floral preservative*

*Glue*

*Gravel*

*Potting soil*

*The Babies Breath and Heather Topiary is an inviting welcome to guests. The babies breath and heather dry beautifully and could be used as a dried design that has been embellished with dried or silk daisies.*

## CREATING THE DESIGN:

Glue the block of dry floral foam into the bottom of the pot. Glue the dry fresh foam block to one end of the tree branch. Soak the foam in preservative-treated water. Glue the other end of the tree branch into the foam in the pot.

Sprinkle about 1" (2.5cm) of gravel on top of the dry floral foam. Add a layer of potting soil on top. Place the ivy plants around the tree branch, filling in with potting soil as needed.

Form a ball shape design, inserting stems of babies breath all around the block of fresh floral foam. Insert the stems of heather in a cluster at the top of the ball of babies breath. The heather will appear to explode from the babies breath.

Randomly insert daisies into the heather cluster and all around the ball of babies breath.

*Dry floral foam, potting soil, and gravel form the base of the topiary design.*

Soil

Gravel

Floral Foam

Clay pot cutaway

# DECORATED POT

## COLLECTING SUPPLIES:

*One 6" (15.2cm) clay pot*
*Basil green floral spray color*
*Hot glue*
*Gold Rub n' Buff®*

## CREATING THE DESIGN:

Drizzle hot glue in a random pattern over the sides of the pot. Spray the pot inside and out with basil color. Allow to dry. Place a small amount of Rub n' Buff® on the end of your finger and gently apply it to the raised areas.

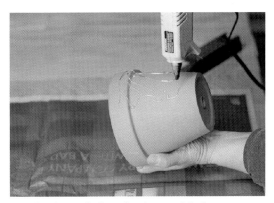

*Randomly apply hot glue in a swirled pattern.*

*Apply Rub n' Buff on the end of your finger to enhance the textural appeal.*

# DINNER PARTY TABLE SETTING

A fresh design with flowers and plants gives life and vitality to any dining experience. This is especially true for an outdoor celebration. The feeling of freshness is carried through to the individual place settings with a surprise cluster of flowers tucked into each napkin.

*Festive fresh flowers and plants enhance an outdoor summer celebration.*

## CENTERPIECE

### COLLECTING SUPPLIES:

*One 14" (35.6cm) long by 7" (17.8cm) wide
x 5" (12.7cm) deep trug style wooden
container with a vine handle*
*Three 4" (10.2cm) African violet plants*
*Four 4" (10.2cm) needlepoint ivy plants
with two or three 12" (30.5cm) long
tendrils*
*5 fresh long-stem yellow roses*
*4 stems fresh white daisy pomps*
*9 water tubes, 5" (12.7cm) long — filled
with preservative filled water*
*4 sweet huck branches — cut 12" to 18"
(30.5cm to 45.7cm) long*
*Florists' foil*
*Potting soil*

### CREATING THE DESIGN:

Line the inside of the container with florists' foil. Position the three violets clustered in the center. Position one ivy plant at each corner of the container. Fill in with potting soil. Create this design so that it can be disassembled after the celebration. Keep the plants in their pots and fill in with potting soil around the pots.

Cut the rose stems 12" (30.5cm), 10" (25.4cm), 9" (22.9cm), 8" (20.3cm) and 7" (17.8cm) long. Insert one rose into each of the water filled tubes. Position the roses in a cluster in the center of the container.

Cut the stems of the daisy pomps shorter than the roses, insert into water filled tubes, and position between the roses. Insert the sweet huck branches in a natural grouping in the center of the design between the flowers.

*Position three violet plants in the center of the container and one ivy in each corner.*

# CANDLES (MAKES ONE)

*Candlelight adds to the ambiance of the affair, while fresh floral napkins welcome each guest.*

## COLLECTING SUPPLIES:

*One 6" x 2" (15.2cm x 5.1cm) candle*
*Approximately nine very slender birch*
*    branches — cut 6" (15.2cm) long*
*Assorted tiny pressed flowers*
*Preserved boxwood*
*Four 18" (45.7cm) long 24 gauge bare*
*    floral wires*
*Wire cutters and floral pruners*
*Brown floral tape*
*White glue*
*Small paint brush*

## CREATING THE DESIGN:

Wrap two of the 24 gauge wires together with the brown floral tape. Repeat with the remaining two wires. Set aside.

Place a small dab of glue at the top of one birch branch. Glue the branch to the candle. Repeat with the remaining branches, positioning them all around the candle. The branches do not require even spacing. After all the branches are in place, wrap one of the taped wires around the top of the candle. Twist to secure. Trim away excess wire. Flatten the wires against the candle. Repeat with the second taped wire to hold the branches at the base of the candle.

Using the paint brush, apply glue to the pressed flowers and greens. Randomly position the flowers and greens all around the sides of the candle between the branches.

# BIRCH CANDLE BASE (MAKES ONE)

## COLLECTING SUPPLIES:

*Birch branches, no larger than 3/8" (.9cm)*
*    diameter — cut 4" to 5" (10.2cm to*
*    12.7cm) long*
*3-1/2" x 4" (8.9cm x 10.2cm) heavy*
*    cardboard*
*Light wood tone floral spray*

## CREATING THE DESIGN:

Spray the front and back of the cardboard with wood tone floral color. Allow to dry.

Glue the branches to the cardboard square to completely cover.

# FOLDED FRESH FLORAL NAPKIN

## COLLECTING SUPPLIES FOR ONE NAPKIN:

*One cloth dinner napkin — color of your choice*
*One fresh yellow rose*
*One white daisy pomp*
*One 3" (7.6cm) stem leatherleaf fern*
*One water tube filled with preservative-treated water*

## CREATING THE DESIGN:

Cut the stems of the rose and daisy 2" (5.1cm) long. Insert the fern, rose, and daisy into the water filled tube.

Open the napkin, fold in half, then half again, forming four squares. Fold diagonally into a triangle. Position the napkin with the four loose corners to the top. Fold the top layer over several times until it forms a cuff at the bottom. Fold the next layer down so that its point touches the cuff. Fold the other two layers on top, with each one shorter than the previous one. Fold the two sides behind and insert the water tube into the center.

*Flowers inserted in water tubes remain fresh for many hours.*

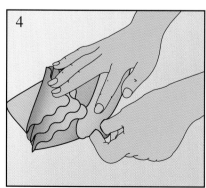

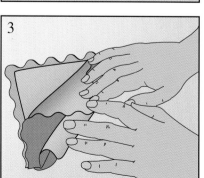

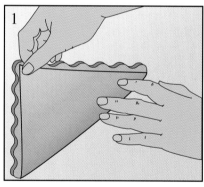

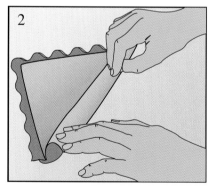

*Folding decorative napkins is easy. This one provides a pocket to showcase flowers.*

# DECORATING CLAY POTS

**A**dding special accents to the containers of a floral arrangement enhances the look and unifies the design. Don't stop here, but following are just a few ideas to get you started. Think about the container of every design you create. Ask yourself how you could add a bit of visual excitement and a touch of magic to an otherwise ordinary container.

*Clay pots take on a whole new look when embellishments and accents are added.*

# BIRDSEED COVERED POT

## COLLECTING SUPPLIES:

*One 4" (10.2cm) clay pot*
*Birdseed*
*Bittersweet stems*
*Two 2-1/2" (6.4cm) mushroom style birds*
*One 3-1/2" (8.9cm) bird nest*
*Three 1" (2.5cm) bird eggs*
*Spanish moss*
*Raffia*
*Thick white glue*
*Small sponge brush*

## CREATING THE DESIGN:

Apply white glue to a section of the clay pot. Roll in birdseed to cover. Repeat, section by section, to entirely cover the pot. Apply a second coat of white glue on top of the birdseed pot to encase the seeds. Tie several lengths of raffia around the pot and add some bittersweet sprigs to the center front.

Place dry floral foam covered with Spanish moss inside the pot. Insert a bittersweet stem into the foam in a natural formation. Glue a bird nest with eggs and a bird near the back of the pot. Glue the second bird in front of the nest.

*Spread white glue on in sections, roll in birdseed, then repeat the process until the pot is covered.*

# POTPOURRI COVERED POT

## COLLECTING SUPPLIES:

*One 4" (10.2cm) clay pot*
*Finely ground potpourri*
*12" (30.5cm) length of 1" (2.5cm) wide*
*    burgundy mesh ribbon*
*Thick white glue*
*Small sponge brush*

## CREATING THE DESIGN:

Apply white glue to a section of the clay pot. Roll in potpourri to cover. Repeat, section by section, to entirely cover the pot. Tie the mesh ribbon around the pot.

# AGED POT

## COLLECTING SUPPLIES:

One 4" (10.2cm) clay pot
Whitewash floral spray
Basil green floral spray color
Soapy water in spray bottle
Small tufts of sheet moss
Glue

## CREATING THE DESIGN:

Saturate the clay pot with soapy water, allowing the water to run freely. Spray with spurts of whitewash, allowing the floral color to run off also. Repeat with the basil floral color in the same manner. Allow to dry. Glue small tufts of sheet moss around the sides of the pot.

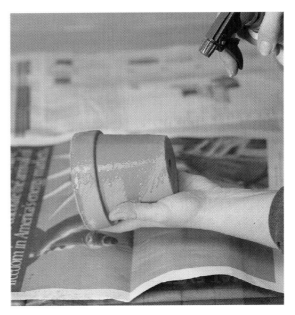

*Fill a spray bottle with water and liquid soap, then shake well before spraying to create an aged look to a pot.*

# LEAF COVERED POT

## COLLECTING SUPPLIES:

One 5" (12.7cm) clay pot
Number of leaves is approximate:
    Twenty 3" (7.6cm) variegated silk
      philodendron leaves
    Fifty 2" (5.1cm) silk rose leaves
    Twenty 1 1/2" (3.8cm) silk rose leaves
    Twenty 1" (2.5cm) silk ivy leaves
White glue

## CREATING THE DESIGN:

Starting at the top of the pot, glue the philodendron leaves around, slightly overlapping them. Allow the leaves to extend 1" (2.5cm) to the inside of the pot.

Entirely cover the rest of the pot with the 2" (5.1cm) silk leaves in the same manner, overlapping the rows. Glue a row of rose leaves just below the rim of the pot. Glue a row of ivy leaves just below the rose leaves. Do not overlap the rows.

Spread a layer of white glue over the completed pot to secure the leaves and add a shiny finish.

*Glue silk leaves in rows, overlapping each other to completely cover a clay pot.*

## GREAT IDEA!

Try other textural items to glue onto your clay pots such as: crushed eggshells, sand, seashells, buttons, beads, and ground spices.

# GARDEN SAMPLER

The idea for this design came from Lydia Huber, one of our designers. Inspired by a needlework sampler, she discussed how she was going to feature each of the flowers in her garden in a sampler that she could enjoy all year. I loved the idea. So here is our inspiration for you to create a memorable floral garden sampler. This design would make a wonderful gift!

All the flowers are pressed. See the Techniques chapter for pressing instructions.

*Showcase your garden's offerings in a pressed sampler.*

## COLLECTING SUPPLIES:

*One 16" x 20" (40.6cm x 50.8cm) wood frame with glass*
*One 16" x 20" (40.6cm x 50.8cm) cardboard*
*One 16" x 20" (40.6cm x 50.8cm) sheet of parchment or mat paper*
*Several sprigs lavender*
*One black-eyed Susan*
*One pansy*
*One daisy*
*One zinnia*
*Several violas*
*Several sprigs heather*
*Several short stems larkspur*
*One Queen Anne's lace*
*2 yards (1.83m) 1/4" (.6cm) wide mauve satin ribbon*
*Moss and several more pressed flowers to embellish the frame*
*Glue*
*Spray adhesive*
*Calligraphy pen and ink*

## CREATING THE DESIGN:

Press the flowers, following directions found in the Techniques section. Glue sheet moss to the top left corner of the frame. Glue a cluster consisting of several sprigs of lavender, heather, larkspur, Queen Anne's lace, black-eyed Susan, and zinnia.

Glue the paper to the cardboard using spray adhesive. Position the flowers on the paper. When positioning, be sure to take into account the space the design on the frame will take up in the finished frame. Glue flowers in place on the paper.

Cut the mauve ribbon to length, forming frames around each of the flowers. Be sure to leave room for the calligraphy. Glue the ribbon in place. Print the corresponding name under each of the flowers. If writing in calligraphy concerns you, rest easy, just print or write the words in your handwriting style.

## GREAT IDEA!

Create miniature sampler squares as stationery by gluing pressed flowers on the front of a note card. Spread a layer of thin white glue over the top of the flowers and the note card. Take care to select the hardiest flowers. Those that are paper thin when pressed work the best.

*Right: The Garden Sampler and Wheat and Rose Candle Design have a clean upscale appearance.*

# WHEAT AND ROSE CANDLE DESIGN

Round rose petals and sharp bearded wheat provide an exciting contrast of textures for this table centerpiece. The colors of these two elements dictate the best display season of the year. For a spectacular autumn design, use yellow roses and orange dyed wheat.

## COLLECTING SUPPLIES:

*One 9" x 2" (22.9cm x 5.1cm) white candle*
*One 6" (15.2cm) clay saucer*
*One 2" (5.1cm) plastic candle holder with*
 *prongs*
*Basil and gold floral color spray*
*One 3-1/2" (8.9cm) square block of dry*
 *floral foam*
*Sheet moss*
*9 dried rose heads*
*Approximately 200 stems dried wheat — cut*
 *in 8" (20.3cm) lengths (measure from*
 *tip to end)*
*15-20 dried or silk ivy leaves*
*20-25 clusters dried mauve pepper berries*
*Rubber glove*
*Glue*
*Wood picks or wire and floral tape*

## CREATING THE DESIGN:

Spray the clay saucer with basil floral color inside and outside. Allow to dry. Spray a small puddle of the gold floral color in the palm of your gloved hand. Using a swiping motion, apply the gold color to the outside of the clay saucer. Allow to dry. Use the same technique to give a gold marbleized finish to the candle. Allow to dry.

Glue the block of foam into the saucer. Cover with a light layer of sheet moss. Place the candle holder in the center of the block of foam. Glue the rose heads all around the candle holder.

Using a wooden pick or wire and floral tape, cluster four wheat stems together. Insert into the foam block under the rose heads. Repeat with the remaining wheat stems, filling in all around the saucer underneath the rose heads. Notice the flared appearance of the wheat in the design. Glue clusters of pepper berries and ivy leaves between the rose heads.

*SPECIAL NOTE:*
*Never leave burning candles unattended.*

*To create an elegant antique look, spray floral color into your gloved hand.*

*Quickly swipe the color in your hand across the surface of the container.*

# GARDEN STONES

Commemorate your family or just add decorative
motifs to garden stones in your personal garden.

**L**eave a lasting remembrance in your garden by carving your family name, important dates or occasions, children's handprints, or simple decorations to enhance the beauty of the setting.

## COLLECTING SUPPLIES:

Garden stones — these can be purchased at
    any garden supply outlet
Dremel® MultiPro™ rotary tool
Silicon carbide grinding stone bit
Dust mask
Safety goggles
Stencil of your choice

## CREATING THE DESIGN:

Be sure the stone is flat and secure. Draw your design with pencil. Use the rotary tool to carve the design into the stone.

## GREAT IDEA!

Create stones featuring your whole family tree complete with handprints, and maybe even footprints! Use the stones on a walkway through your garden.

A stencil makes a wonderful pattern and is easily
transferred with a pencil.

Trace the outline with a rotary tool.

Use container gardens near your front door to make a statement using just one type of flower or creating a colorful mix of several types.

Wind chimes add a delightful sound to a deck or patio setting.

Use container gardens to liven up a plain concrete patio. Place several together for greater impact. Use steps and benches for height.

To hold fresh plants and flowers, use a hollowed out log, old watering can, antique chair, or wicker picnic basket.

In place of a windsock, tie two simple loop bows of 2" (5.1cm) wide ribbons in coordinating colors and patterns around a grapevine wreath. The ribbon lengths should be cut approximately 1-1/2 yards (1.37m) long. Hang the wreath on your patio or front porch, allowing the streamers to sway in the breeze. Add jingle bells for a musical touch.

Use an old swing set, colorfully painted, to create a place to hang a variety of basket style planters.

Give flowers a second life, allowing the memories to continue. Remove flowers from the vase, bouquet, or arrangement just before they wilt and die. Wrap a rubber band around the stems of a same flower bunch. Hang them upside-down in a warm dry location and allow them to dry naturally. They will become brittle and their color tone may deepen. Handle with care. Incorporate them into a dried floral design for a special place in your home and allow their memories to live.

Tuck a single perfect rose in a water filled tube into the briefcase or suitcase of someone special on the day of a big meeting or important trip. Add a short message such as "Good luck," "I'm thinking of you," or "Sleep tight."

Dry flowers from special occasions and use for wreaths or glass domed designs.

Slice lemons, limes, or oranges into a bowl of cold water. Rinse the slices well to remove acid. Add some of the slices to a clear glass container half filled with cold water. Place an arrangement of fresh flowers into the container. Add more slices around the flower stems. Finish filling the vase with more cold water.

# PART FIVE
# Herbs & Potpourri

The first time I visited England, I was surprised to find that nearly everywhere I looked, there sat a small basket of potpourri. They were placed on the counters and toilet backs in restrooms. There was a basket on my nightstand at the hotel and in several places in the lobby. They were also in the restroom on the train, in the postal office, the grocery store, and the department stores. The home of every family I visited had numerous bowls and baskets of potpourri tucked around and through their homes. In some cases, the aroma of the potpourri was especially lovely. In other cases, it no longer had any aroma at all — it just looked warm and inviting.

My first visit was a result of demonstrations I presented at Douthwaite's Florist Sundries in Leeds. It was during this first visit that I met an extraordinary individual named Kathleen Bretherick. She has helped me at every one of my British presentations since that first year. Kath, as she calls herself, is a retired florist. Her daughter Sandra still runs the two Bretherick's florist shops today. Kath was involved in all aspects of British floristry. For many years she held numerous offices and holds the honor of awards being given in her name. It was with Kath's coaxing and sponsorship that I was among the first Americans to be selected as a member of the Society of Floristry in England.

One of the things I remember most about Kath is her home. She lives in a townhouse on the grounds of the old Harewood estate. Her back yard is walled in and is not very large. However, the variety of beautiful flowers and herbs she is able to grow is absolutely amazing. The whole yard looks like a botanical garden. The birds and squirrels love it and visit often because she leaves appropriate foods for them. She has a small sitting room that overlooks this marvelous space. Over a cup of good English tea, we sat there that first time and talked about the differences between America and England. I watched her lavender blowing in the wind and commented. She then shared with me all the wonderful things that are done with lavender in England.

I often receive a packet from Kath filled with newsy letters, photos of her newest designs, and sometimes a little memento from her travels. One day I opened another Kath Bretherick packet to find a beautiful sachet filled with sweet smelling lavender. When I turned it over, the attached note said, "This was made with the first lavender from my garden. Love, Kath." I used it all through the year in my drawer and often reminisced as I caught the lavender scent on a garment I was wearing. She has sent a few more since then and I treasure every one as I treasure her love and friendship. I often think of her when I smell lavender.

Can you touch the life of someone you love today with the beauty and aroma of herbs and potpourri?

# PREPARING HERBS AND POTPOURRI

## HERBS

Ancient cultures cultivated herbs for their healing properties. Mixtures of dried flowers and herbs were used early in history to mask unpleasant odors. Through the years, the therapeutic qualities of herbs have been used to cure illness and lift the spirit. Herbs have been valued for their medicinal and cosmetic properties.

Today, you can find many herbs and herbal preparations readily available at the local supermarket, bath shop, or health store. There has been a renewed interest in growing herbs to use for herbal teas, aromatherapy, and cosmetic purposes.

Herbs are among the easiest plants to grow. Once established, they need little attention. Although they will grow mixed in with a variety of other plants, it is best to stake out a small area designed just for growing herbs. Herbs grow in normal garden soil, which is a balanced mixture of clay, humus, lime, and sand.

Leafy herbs should be harvested on a dry day just before the plant begins to flower. It is at this stage when the volatile oils contained in the leaves are at their highest. The flavor, color, and scent of the herbs depend on the abundance of volatile oils.

Gather flowering herbs such as rosemary, hyssop, thyme, lavender, and mugwort when the flowers are just beginning to open. Collect flowers and petals when the flowers are fully open. Do this on a daily basis to ensure the flower is picked at its peak.

Air drying is the easiest method of drying herbs at home. To air dry herbs, simply bundle a combination of eight or more of one variety of stems. Tie the stems together with a rubber band or twine. Always dry herbs in the dark, hanging upside-down in a dry warm space. Depending on the type of herb, drying time may take from four days to three weeks. Do not over dry. You can test to see if they are ready simply by touching them. All the moisture should be out of the stems and leaves.

Herb leaves can be dried in a microwave oven. Herb flowers do not dry easily using this method. Remove the leaves from their stems. Place them in a single layer on a paper towel. Microwave on high for thirty seconds. Turn the leaves over and microwave thirty seconds to one minute more, checking at five second intervals to see if they are completely dry.

When storing dried herbs, strip the leaves from their stems and place them in glass jars or fabric bags. Label carefully and store in a dark place.

To preserve herbs or leaves for design work, place them in a vase or container filled with a mixture of two parts warm water to one part glycerin. For better absorption of the solution, cut several diagonal slits in the submerged stems. The result of this process will be a softer, more life-like product.

## POTPOURRI

The art of making potpourri dates back long before the time of the pharaohs. Historically, it was used to mask odors from poor sanitation as well as to ward off insects. The word potpourri translates from French to mean "rotten pot." Today, potpourri is simply a mixture of dried flowers and other ingredients used to add fragrance to a room.

The basic ingredients for potpourri are: fragrant flowers, leaves, herbs, spices, colorful blossoms, fixatives to hold the fragrance, and essential oils.

Some fragrant flowers that are lovely to include are roses, marigolds, jasmine, carnations, anemones, scented geraniums, and peonies. Foliage such as eucalyptus and bay leaves also have distinctive scents. The pungent fragrance of herbal chamomile, feverfew, lavender, lemon verbena, sage, rosemary, artemisia, thyme, basil, and mint are pleasant additions to a potpourri mixture as well as spicy cinnamon, star anise, clove, mace, and nutmeg.

Give your potpourri a vibrant look with bachelor buttons, zinnias, globe amaranth, salvia, delphiniums, pansies, and violets. Dried peels from lemons, limes, oranges, and grapefruit add interesting texture and color.

Fixatives, which help retain the aroma of the oils include orris root powder, ground gum benzoin, and crumbled cinnamon sticks. Also use oil of sandalwood, clove, or patchouli. A rule of thumb is to use a tablespoon of fixative for every cup of dried materials. Essential oil is the pure oil of a flower, spice, or herb. All ingredients contribute to the blend but the essential oil dominates the potpourri mixture. Use only a few drops at a time. More can be added as the fragrance dissipates. Never use essential oils directly on the skin or take them internally.

When making potpourri, all materials must be crispy dry. Do not use plastic bowls or utensils as they tend to absorb the fragrance. Gently mix all the dry ingredients together. Next, use an eye dropper to scatter drops of essential oil over the combined mixture. Seal the mixture in an airtight container. Stir or shake every two days. Allow to cure for four to six weeks before displaying.

If you are a true potpourri enthusiast, you may want to plant a potpourri garden. Spring is the best time. Grow plants in a rectangular bed, bordered in front of shrubs, in a window box, patio container, and on a sunny windowsill indoors. Most plants enjoy the full sun and require shelter from the wind.

Harvest potpourri flowers late on a sunny morning after the night moisture has evaporated. Air drying is the easiest. Bundle like materials together. Hang upside-down in a dark, dry place with good air circulation. Most will dry within a week or two.

Don't have time to make your own? There are many varieties and combinations available in retail stores. Simply choose the color or scent you like and attractively display it in a beautiful container.

Brass, copper, crystal, crockery, or wooden containers, along with baskets, jars, and dishes are suitable vessels for display. If you do not have a large amount of potpourri, fill the bottom of your container with moss, excelsior, or crumpled paper, placing the potpourri on top. For something a little different, create a design of layered potpourri, moss, and colorful dried flowers in a tall clear vase.

# HERBAL BATH CARE

*Luxurious oils can be stored in interestingly shaped bottles with natural embellishments.*

Scent can soothe and relax. Add ingredients to the bath to restore moisture in the skin as well as soften and perfume the water. Add no more than a teaspoon for a full bath and swish your hand though the water, distributing the oil evenly before getting in the tub. When using herbal oils as a gift, always include a label or note to explain the materials in the mixture and how best to use the creation.

# DECORATING BOTTLES

## COLLECTING SUPPLIES:

*One bottle — size, color, and shape of your
    choice*
*Paraffin*
*Old tin tuna fish can*
*Double boiler*
*Hot glue*

## MATERIALS TO EMBELLISH BOTTLES:

Thin natural ribbons and cording
Natural raffia
Wheat
Pennyroyal
Assortment of very small pods
Dried orange, kiwi, and apple slices
Artemisia
Eucalyptus
Dried rosebuds
Globe amaranth

Fill the bottle with the prepared oil of your choice. Replace the cork
firmly. In the top of the double boiler, put the block of paraffin in the can
and place it in an inch of water. When the wax just melts, turn the bottle
over and dip the neck into the wax. Remove and let cool for a minute,
then re-dip and remove. Continue to dip, remove and cool until a thick
coating of wax covers the cork and the neck of the bottle.

Glue on the embellishments of your choice, trying to tie the embellishments into the theme or scent of the contents of the bottle.

## GREAT IDEA!

Multi-looped bows, using narrow ribbon of different texture combinations, give a striking accented look to the bottled designs. Add a
natural or masculine look with raffia or twine. Lacy ribbons will
evoke a feminine feeling.

# BATH OILS

Use almond, safflower, or sunflower oil as a base ingredient. Mix proportions as needed to fill the bottles of your choice. Here are two recipes to get you started.

## TO REFRESH AND STIMULATE:

1 cup almond oil
8 drops lemon oil
8 drops peppermint oil

## TO SOOTHE AND RELAX:

1 cup almond oil
10 drops lavender oil
6 drops rose oil

When creating bath oil recipes, a rule of thumb is to use one drop of essential oil to three tablespoons of oil or honey. Leave for a few days so the scent will develop. Use about a teaspoon per bath.

# HERBAL BATH TEA BAGS

At the end of a stressful day, I love to take comfort in a hot bath. To enhance the relaxation process, I turn off the lights in the bathroom and light a candle or two on the edge of the bathtub. I play soft music in the room as I relax, watch the candle, and rejuvenate. I might add an herbal bath tea to the water. They make welcome companions that soothe and comfort a weary body at the end of the day. These fragrant bags, candlelight, a warm cup of tea, and soft music combine beautifully and I instantly feel the stress of the day disappear.

## COLLECTING SUPPLIES:

*Muslin, cheesecloth, organdy, or gauze fabric*
*Either fresh or dried herbs can be used*
*Combine:*
*comfrey and chamomile*
*or*
*lemon verbena, thyme, and peppermint*
*or*
*chamomile, lavender, and thyme*
*or*
*yarrow, fennel, sage, and rosemary*
*or*
*lavender and dried rosebuds*
*or*
*use any one of these herbs by itself*
*Needle and thread*

## CREATING THE DESIGN:

Cut two 4" (10.2cm) squares of fabric with pinking shears. Stitch three sides together using a 1/4" to 1/2" (.6cm to 1.3cm) seam allowance. Fill with herb combinations as suggested. Stitch closed.

You can also make these bags with one 6" to 8" (15.2cm to 20.3cm) square of fabric. Place the herbs in the center of the fabric, bring up all the sides and tie closed with a string.

Place whichever style of tea bag you choose into the tub and leave to soak in the water or hold under the faucet while filling the tub. Use different mixtures of herbs to provide a variety of effects. The effect of the herbs weakens with each bath. However, if you hang and dry them after each bath, they can be used more than once.

## GREAT IDEA!

Add a small amount of oatmeal to the herb mixture to give your skin a silky feeling.

*Herbal tea bags can add fragrance to a relaxing bath.*

# STRESS RELIEF TUBE

**G**ive your spouse or dad a special treat by making him this simple, tension reducing tube to use just about anywhere on the body. It makes a great gift for Father's Day. Heat it in the microwave to produce its relaxing effect.

## COLLECTING SUPPLIES:

*Fabric of your choice, 13" x 1 yard
(33cm x .91m)
1 lb. large pearl tapioca
1-1/2 lbs. long grain rice (not instant)
Peppermint essential oil
Plastic funnel — cut the opening slightly
larger so the rice and tapioca will fit
through the spout
Needle and thread*

*Warm the Stress Relief Tube in the microwave, then sit back and relax as you enjoy the deep healing heat it provides.*

## CREATING THE DESIGN:

Fold the fabric in half lengthwise, right sides together. Using a 1/2" (1.3cm) seam allowance, stitch across the bottom and up the side to form a long tube. Turn the tube right side out.

Use a triple zigzag stitch, at 2" (5.1cm) intervals to sew up the length of the tube. This will create three chambers.

Mix the tapioca and rice together. Sprinkle with a few drops of peppermint oil. Using the funnel, fill each of the cham-

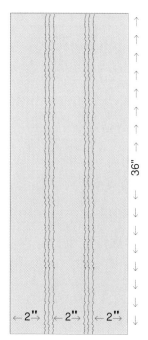

36"

←2"→ ←2"→ ←2"→

*Sew three long pockets using a triple zigzag stitch to hold the rice and tapioca mixture.*

bers with the rice and tapioca mixture. Turn the top edge over and slipstitch closed.

To use, place the collar in the microwave for two to three minutes on high. (Times may vary in different microwave ovens.) Do not overheat. The collar will stay warm for fifteen to twenty minutes.

*Use a funnel for pouring the rice and tapioca mixture into the pockets of the tube.*

# FRESH FLORAL POTPOURRI BASKET

A combination of potpourri and fresh flowers creates a fabulously fragrant centerpiece for your kitchen. Use colors to coordinate with the setting.

## COLLECTING SUPPLIES:

*Wicker basket, approximately 12" (30.5cm) long by 8" (20.3cm) wide and 6" (15.2cm) deep — color of your choice*
*1/3 block fresh floral foam*
*Plastic liner, container, or sheet of florists' foil to hold wet foam*
*8 stems fresh white monte casino*
*8 stems fresh yellow freesia*
*8 stems fresh lavender crown asters*
*4 lemons*
*Several dried orange and kiwi slices*
*Potpourri — use a color to blend with the flowers*
*Spanish moss*
*4" (10.2cm) long wooden picks*
*Fresh floral preservative*
*Glue*

## CREATING THE DESIGN:

Soak the foam in floral preservative treated water. Wedge into the waterproof liner or line the basket with florists' foil. Place the foam into the left side of the basket as close to the edge as possible. Fill the right of the basket with Spanish moss approximately 2" (5.1cm) from the top of the basket edge. Tuck the

*The floral foam is situated in one half of the basket.*

*Stems of monte casino form the shape of the floral design.*

*The lovely fragrance of potpourri and fresh flowers combine in this striking design. Crown asters add shape, visual weight, and a touch of color.*

moss around but do not cover the foam.

Starting with the monte casino, insert the stems into the foam, forming a casual arrangement of flowers. Fill in with stems of freesia and crown asters.

Insert the wooden picks into the lemons. Cluster them in the front of the design. Glue the orange and kiwi slices around and between the lemons.

Sprinkle the potpourri over the moss on the right side of the basket.

# POTPOURRI BOXES, LAYERED POTPOURRI AND LAVENDER PIN CUSHION

*Potpourri can be displayed in a number of ways to enhance a room.*

**M**y friend from England, Kath Bretherick, told me about this style of pin cushion. Her inspiration made me want to create one of my own. Each time a pin is inserted, the wonderful fragrance of lavender escapes.

I have included the pin cushion in a grouping of potpourri filled containers to set a nostalgic mood that coordinates with my family pictures. I treasure each of these "old-time" looking pictures taken with my sons over the years.

# LAVENDER PIN CUSHION

## COLLECTING SUPPLIES:

One 3-1/2" (8.9cm) floral printed cardboard
   box with lid
6" (15.2cm) circle of fabric to coordinate
   with the box
1 cup dried lavender buds
15" (38.1cm) of 3/4" (1.9cm) wide
   decorative fabric trimming

## CREATING THE DESIGN:

Glue approximately 1/4" (.6cm) of the
fabric tightly over the top side edge of the
box lid. Gather slightly if needed. Fill with
the lavender buds. Glue another small section. Add more lavender. Continue until
you have a nicely rounded firm covering.
Glue the fabric securely over the lavender
buds. Trim the fabric if necessary. Glue the
decorative trimming over the cut edge of
the fabric around the side of the box lid.

Another suggestion is to use a mixture
of rosebuds and petals, lavender, rosemary,
and crushed cinnamon sticks to fill a pin
cushion.

# STACKED FLORAL BOXES

## COLLECTING SUPPLIES:

One 6" (15.2cm) and one 4-1/2" (11.4cm)
   floral printed box with lid
4 dried rose heads
4 small dried hydrangea clusters — If the
   color of the hydrangea blossoms has
   faded, gently mist the flowers with a
   combination of hyacinth and dusty rose
   floral spray color to rejuvenate their
   natural look.
1-1/4 yards (1.14m) of 1-1/2" (3.8cm) wide
   lavender striped ribbon — cut two 5"
   (12.7cm) lengths and one 35" (88.9cm)
   length
1-1/2 yards (1.37m) of 3/8" (.9cm) wide
   mauve satin picot edge ribbon
1-1/2 yards (1.37m) of 1/4" (.6cm) wide
   lavender satin picot edge ribbon
Small amount potpourri

## CREATING THE DESIGN:

Stack the two boxes on top of each
other. Tie them together with the 35"
(88.9cm) length of ribbon. Form a layered
bow with the
two picot
edged ribbons.
Glue the bow
to the center of
the lid of the
smaller box.
Glue the roses
and hydrangea
clusters
between the
bow loops.
Fold one of the
5" (12.7cm)
lengths of lav-
ender striped ribbon in half. Stitch or glue
the sides of the folded ribbon, leaving the
top open to form a sachet. Fill 3/4 full of
potpourri. Tie with a 4" (10.2cm) length of
the 1/4" (.6cm) wide lavender ribbon. Form
a second sachet in the same manner and tie
to the streamers cascading over the side of
the boxes.

# LARGE BOX WITH POTPOURRI

## COLLECTING SUPPLIES:

One 7-1/2" (19.1cm) floral printed box with lid
One dried rose head
12 dried petite chive flower clusters — cut 1-1/2" (3.8cm) long
12 dried royal crown flowers — cut 1-1/2" (3.8cm) long
12 dried mauve pepper berry clusters — cut 1-1/2" (3.8cm) long
12 dried pink ti tree clusters — cut 1-1/2" (3.8cm) long
Glue
Potpourri

## CREATING THE DESIGN:

Glue the rose head to the center of the lid. Using one type of dried material at a time, form a cluster of flowers around the rose, equally spacing the colors and textures.

Fill the box with a coordinating color of potpourri.

# LAYERED POTPOURRI VASE

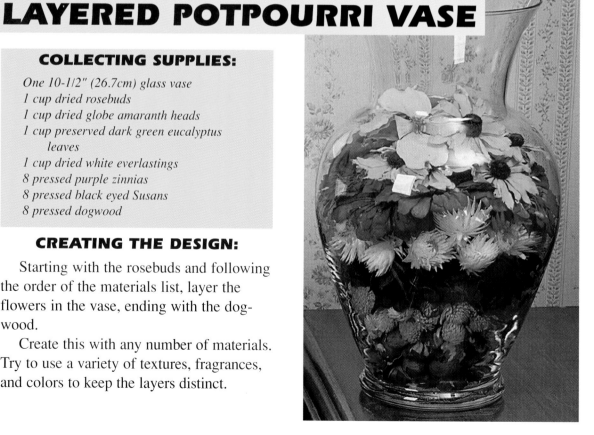

## COLLECTING SUPPLIES:

One 10-1/2" (26.7cm) glass vase
1 cup dried rosebuds
1 cup dried globe amaranth heads
1 cup preserved dark green eucalyptus leaves
1 cup dried white everlastings
8 pressed purple zinnias
8 pressed black eyed Susans
8 pressed dogwood

## CREATING THE DESIGN:

Starting with the rosebuds and following the order of the materials list, layer the flowers in the vase, ending with the dogwood.

Create this with any number of materials. Try to use a variety of textures, fragrances, and colors to keep the layers distinct.

# POTPOURRI CAKES AND CUPCAKES

*Come to a tea party, complete with everlasting cakes and cupcakes.*

An invitation to high-tea anyone? These no-fat, no-calorie creations are striking decorations for your next party or shower. Use the smaller designs as favors and the larger items as table decorations. Your party guests will have to look twice to see if they are real!

# COCONUT EVERLASTING CAKE

## CREATING THE DESIGN:

Glue the discs together. Glue the Spanish moss to cover the sides of the discs. Gently mist the moss with the flat white floral color until the moss resembles coconut.

Spray the salal leaves with gold floral color. Allow to dry. Gently mist with the flat white floral color. To "frost" the cake, start at the outside edge of the top disc and glue the salal leaves side-by-side (not overlapping) to cover the top. Glue an outside row and an inside row in this manner flat against the top disc. Glue two more rows on top of the leaves, positioning them between the previous rows to completely cover the cake.

Use the everlastings to trim all around the top outside edge of the cake. Do the same with the pepper berry clusters around the bottom outside edge of the cake.

In the center of the cake, create a garnish of three everlastings, three hedera leaves, and three pepper berry clusters. Add the six orange halves equally spaced around the center cluster of flowers.

Finish trimming the cake with ten clusters, each with three rosebuds and one hedera leaf, equally spaced around the top edge of the cake.

*A symmetrical design created with leaves, roses, orange slices, and pepper berries complete the top of this striking cake.*

# GERMAN CHOCOLATE CAKE

*A German chocolate look-alike cake is easy to create.*

## COLLECTING SUPPLIES:

*One block dry floral foam, 4" (10.2cm)
     square by 2" (5.1cm) high*
*2 cups cloves*
*30 dried globe amaranth heads*
*3 dried rosebuds*
*Small amount black lichen moss*
*3 dried bay leaves*
*Natural reindeer moss*
*Glue*

## CREATING THE DESIGN:

Cover the floral foam lightly with reindeer moss. Coat with a layer of cloves. Use the amaranth heads to trim around the side of the tart. In the center, garnish with a cluster of rosebuds, bay leaves, and black lichen moss.

*A good base for faux cakes is dry floral foam and a layer of reindeer moss.*

# LAYERED STRAWBERRY CAKE

## COLLECTING SUPPLIES:

One 4" (10.2 cm) triangle of dry floral
   foam — round corners slightly
Natural reindeer moss
2 cups pink larkspur blossoms
One half freeze-dried, silk, or plastic
   strawberry
3 stems deep red yarrow
Approximately 100 white hill flower heads
Approximately 15 white lagurus heads
Glue

## CREATING THE DESIGN:

Lightly cover the floral foam with reindeer moss. On two sides of the foam triangle, in one continuous line, trim with the hill flowers and yarrow to resemble strawberry and cream filling.

Cover the rest of the cake slice with the larkspur flower heads. Garnish with a cluster of the lagurus heads, a strawberry half, and three hedera leaves. Create these to look like a dollop of whipped cream topped off with a strawberry.

# BLACKBERRY CREAM CAKE

## COLLECTING SUPPLIES:

Two 3-1/2" x 1" (8.9cm x 2.5cm) foam discs
18 freeze-dried, silk, or plastic blackberries
One Queen Anne's lace pressed flower head
18 white hill flower heads
12 hedera berry leaves
4 red amaranthus — cut 3" (7.6cm) long
Ivory floral color spray
Glue

## CREATING THE DESIGN:

Glue the two discs together. Cover the top and sides of the discs with the berry leaves. Spray the ivory floral color over the leaves to completely cover. Allow to dry.

Garnish the top of the cake with an edging of blackberries and the pressed Queen Anne's lace flower. Trim the bottom edge with a row of amaranthus and then equally space the hill flowers around.

# CUPCAKES

## COLLECTING SUPPLIES FOR ONE CUPCAKE:

*Gold foil cupcake liner*
*1" (2.5cm) square block dry floral foam*
*Dried oregano or babies breath — cut into*
*    1" to 2" (2.5cm to 5.1cm) long pieces*
*Pressed pansy or preserved berries*

## CREATING THE DESIGN:

Glue the foam block into the liner. Insert the stems of the chosen dried materials into the foam to form a mound. Garnish with a pressed flower or berries.

*A small block of foam glued into a cupcake liner forms the base for floral cupcakes.*

# POTPOURRI PILLOW

This idea came to me from my sister Diane. She saves the flowers her daughter Danielle receives, then dries or presses them and adds them to her memory pillow. This pillow contains all the flowers Danielle has ever received. It is a wonderful memento of all the special times in her life. Diane also keeps a log listing what celebrations the flowers commemorate. Create this gift and give it to your daughter on her wedding day!

## COLLECTING SUPPLIES:

*One 16" (40.6cm) square ivory pillow with a ruffle*
*14" (35.6cm) square sheer ivory organdy*
*1-3/4 yard (1.6m) of 1/4" (.6cm) wide mauve/gold roping*
*Six 2" (5.1cm) silk rose leaves*
*Eight 1" (2.5cm) mauve silk alstroemeria flower heads*
*1-3/8 yard (1.26m) of 3/8" (.9cm) wide mauve satin picot edge ribbon*
*1 yard (.91m) of 3/8" (.9cm) wide blue satin picot edge ribbon*
*Dried flower petals, leaves, and pressed flowers*
*1 yard (.91m) of 1/4" (.6cm) wide ivory Velcro® closure*
*Waxed paper*
*Glue*

## CREATING THE DESIGN:

Leaving a 1/4" (.6cm) seam allowance, cut the organdy to fit inside the pillow's ruffled edge. Fold the organdy over 1/4" (.6cm) and stitch or glue all around to finish the ends.

Cut the Velcro® to fit one side of the organdy square. Glue one part of the Velcro to the edge of the organdy square that will be positioned at the top of the pillow edge. Glue the other side of the Velcro to the pillow at the top edge.

Place the organdy on a waxed paper

*Save dried and pressed flowers from special occasions and display them in a decorative pillow.*

covered surface for this step. With the Velcro at the top, start at the bottom left corner of the organdy square and glue the strips of picot edge ribbon in a fan design, alternating the colors.

Attach the organdy square to the pillow by gluing the three non-Velcro sides to the square. Match the Velcro sides together. Start at the bottom left corner and glue the roping all around. Cover the edge of the organdy. Glue the cluster of leaves and flower heads to the bottom left corner of the pillow.

Gently fill the pocket with dried flower leaves and petals.

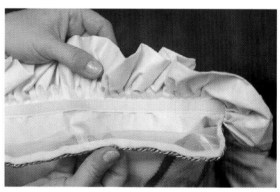

*Using Velcro on one side allows you to add more flowers at any time.*

# POTPOURRI RECIPES

## LAVENDER POTPOURRI

1 cup lavender flowers
1/8 cup larkspur petals
1/8 cup cornflower petals
1 tsp. powdered orris root
2 drops lavender essential oil

Mix the flowers and orris root together. Add the essential oil. Place in a paper bag or sealed container and allow to cure for four to six weeks. Occasionally stir or shake the contents.

## A SIMPLE ROSE MIXTURE POTPOURRI

1 pint dried roses
1 oz. mixed herbs
1/2 oz. orris root powder
1 crumbled cinnamon stick

1/2 tsp. cloves
1 star anise
Orange peel
2 drops rose oil
1 drop lavender oil

## MIXED GARDEN POTPOURRI

2 cups dried mixed flower petals
5 tbs. mixed spices and herbs
1/2 oz. orris root powder
4 drops essential oil of your choice

## FRAGRANT POTPOURRI

1/4 cup rose petals
1/4 cup yarrow
1/4 cup peppermint
1/4 cup lavender
1/4 cup crushed cinnamon sticks
1/4 cup pennyroyal
1/4 cup cloves

## GREAT IDEA!

Another friend of mine, Barb Kessing, has taken all of her daughter Amy's dried corsages from dances and proms and attached them to a wreath to hang in Amy's room.

# HERBAL WREATH

*Colors, textures, and styles of herbs combine to create a wreath that can be enjoyed all year.*

I love the fragrance of herbs. On a bright summer day, fond childhood memories awaken when I catch the gentle scent of peppermint floating on the breeze. Bay leaves simmering in a pot of chicken soup remind me of my grandmother's kitchen.

You can experience the pleasure of herbs by growing your own and then drying them to use for cooking or decoration. I have created this herbal wreath design so I can enjoy their fragrance year round. It is a perfect accent for a kitchen or active living area in your home.

Use any combination of herbs. Consider colors, textures, and fragrances when planning your design. Use rosemary for remembrance, sage for virtue, and globe amaranth for everlasting affection to create a symbolic wedding wreath.

*Ribbon is woven on the back of the herbal wreath to stop the eye of the viewer, allowing the design to be contained and enjoyed.*

## COLLECTING SUPPLIES:

One 16" (40.6cm) straw wreath

2 yards (1.83m) 4" (10.2cm) wide sheer
 sage green ribbon

1-1/2 yards (1.37m) of 1-3/4" (4.4cm) wide
 mesh rust ribbon

2 yards (1.83m) natural twine

Approximately 100 stems each of the
 following dried materials — cut in 3"
 to 4" (7.6cm to 10.2cm) lengths:
   oregano
   artemisia
   nigella

Approximately 50 stems of the following
 dried materials — cut in 3" to 4"
 (7.6cm to 10.2cm) lengths
   globe thistles
   tansy
   yellow statice
   globe amaranth

Approximately 6 to 8 stems each of the
 following dried materials:
  yarrow — cut 15" (38.1cm) long
  lamb's ear — cut 15" (38.1cm) long
  meadow mint — cut 18" (45.7cm) long
  preserved choctaw foliage — cut 18"
  (45.7cm) long

"U" shaped floral pins

32 gauge wire

## CREATING THE DESIGN:

Cut the sheer sage ribbon into six 15" (38.1cm) lengths. Set the remaining 1-1/2 yard (1.37m) length aside. Use the 15" (38.1cm) lengths to create a lattice effect across the back of the wreath. Secure three lengths vertically with floral pins. Weave the three remaining lengths horizontally, securing in the same manner.

Form a cluster of six to eight stems of oregano. Use a floral pin to secure this cluster to the outside edge of the wreath. Repeat with clusters of nigella and artemisia, overlapping each cluster over the previous one. Continue this pattern to cover the outside edge.

Repeat this method to cover the inside edge of the wreath with clusters of nigella, statice, and artemisia. Equally space six clusters of globe thistles around the center top of the wreath. Fill in with clusters of tansy, oregano, and globe amaranth around the wreath.

Starting with the choctaw foliage, layer the stems of mint, then lamb's ear and yarrow on top of each other to form a larger cluster. It should measure approximately 18" (45.7cm) long from the tips of the foliage to the end of the stems. Secure with a short length of wire.

Create a layered bow using the remaining 1-1/2 yards (1.37 meters) of the sheer ribbon, 1-1/2 yards (1.37 meters) of mesh ribbon, and the 2 yards (1.83 meters) of the natural twine. Secure at the base of the large cluster of dried materials. Attach to the bottom center of the wreath. Allow the ribbon streamers to cascade down.

## GREAT IDEA!

Without the center cluster of materials, this wreath is an effective candle ring. Simply place it flat on the table. Use the bow attached to the top of the ring with streamers cascading. In the center, use either one tall fat candle or several taper candles. Be sure to watch the candles carefully and do not let them burn too close to the dried materials and never leave candles burning unattended.

# INSECT REPELLENT SWAG

Create a cluster of scented herbs to hang on the back of a door or in a closet. This is an old fashioned method to chase away insects. These materials can be fresh to begin with, allowing them to dry over several weeks. Artemisia, peppermint, and lavender are particularly effective.

Artemisia has a bitter scent that will ward off insects. Peppermint will ward off mice. Lavender will keep stored linens and clothes fresh smelling.

You can add dried roses or other colorful materials to make the swag more attractive.

## COLLECTING SUPPLIES:

*2-1/2 yards (2.29m) of 2-1/2" (6.4cm) wide sheer moss green ribbon*
*2-1/2 yards (2.29m) of 1-1/2" (3.8cm) wide metallic gold mesh ribbon*
*Six 1 yard (.91m) lengths natural raffia*
*All of the following dried materials are 24" (61cm) long*
   *50 stems penny royal*
   *40 stems tansy*
   *30 stems lavender*
   *20 stems red yarrow*
   *10 stems yellow yarrow*
*32 gauge wire*

## CREATING THE DESIGN:

Layer the dried materials on top of each other as follows, starting with the back of the swag:  penny royal, tansy, lavender, red yarrow, and yellow yarrow. Secure the cluster together with a short length of wire approximately 3" (7.6cm) below the yellow yarrow. Cut the stems even. The cluster should measure approximately 24" (61cm) long

Form a layered bow with the sheer ribbon, raffia, and metallic ribbon. Attach to the cluster. Allow the bow streamers to cascade on each side of the dried materials.

*The scents of many herbs are useful for warding off bugs and insects.*

## GREAT IDEA!

To create an effective moth repellent, combine 1/2 cup dried lavender, 1/4 cup crushed cinnamon sticks, and 1/2 tsp. whole black peppercorns. Use the mixture in small sachets.

❖ Form a bunch of 100 or more lavender stems, keeping the flower heads even. Tie together securely halfway between the flowers and the ends of the stems. Cut the stems so they are perfectly even at the bottom of the bunch so the bunch will stand by itself. As a finishing touch, tie a pretty ribbon around it.

❖ Make small fabric sachets from scraps of fabric. Stitch or tie closed with a floral ribbon. Use herb mixtures to scent clothes and linens as well as keeping insects away. A mixture of 4 tsp. tansy, 4 tsp. artemisia, 2 tsp. lavender, 1 tsp. rosemary, and 1/2 tsp. powdered orris root can be used as an insect repellent.

❖ Use a fresh bunch of mint or lilac by an open window to keep flies away.

❖ Use a long oblong container that will fit on a window sill and hold three herb plants. Line the inside with florists' foil or plastic. Plant three of the same or different herb plants. Keep the soil moist and feed with a liquid fertilizer. Shelter from direct sunlight. Nip the flower buds to induce more leaf production. Basil, parsley, and chives thrive indoors and outside.

❖ Tie bunches of fresh herbs on napkins for a special occasion dinner party.

❖ Use small clusters of herbs as a package tie. Spray them with gold to use on holiday packages.

❖ Use clusters or small garlands of dried herbs for decorative curtain tie backs.

❖ For a summer place setting, use a garland of fresh herbs to decorate around the dinner plate.

❖ Cover a straw wreath of any size with 4" (10.2cm) long bunches of fresh herbs attached with floral pins. Use lavender, fennel, sage, oregano, yarrow, chives, peppermint, and goldenrod. The herbs will dry in about two weeks.

# PART SIX
# Harvest

Autumn is a truly abundant time of year when the fruit is heavy on the trees, the harvest almost home, and the fiery show of brilliant colors couples with the incredible textures of natural materials. It is a season that is overflowing with riches in sound, sight, smell, taste, and touch — an incredible multi-sensory experience.

As you walk through the woods in search of treasures, think about the rustle of the leaves. Remember the sound of screams and laughter as you rake a huge pile of leaves, then jump in it and drag others to join you.

Remember the brilliant colors and flamboyant fall blooms in yellows and golds, oranges and rusts, and every shade of green and red imaginable.

Probably my favorite memory of fall is the smell of fresh apples and hot apple pie. When we were younger, my parents would take us to a small shack on a huge parcel of land filled with apple trees. We would buy bushels of apples, then bring them home to make apple pie, apple sauce, and apple butter. The apples were the best around. As the years went by, the shack turned into a small hut making way for a storefront. This storefront later turned into a sprawling complex, complete with a florist shop, ice cream hut, bakery, restaurant, and produce market.

We try to continue to visit each year to get our fill of apples. We are now able to view the operation from a visitors' deck. We actually see the huge vats of apples being cleaned, sorted and bagged. It is very different from the little shack I remember from my youth, but interestingly, the aromas and tastes remain the same.

Another fond memory I have of the autumn season is our yearly pumpkin carving experience. We take this very seriously as we hunt for the perfect carving pumpkin in the many fields around our home. When we select the pumpkins, we try to imagine what type of face this particular one will sport. Some are funny, others serious, some scary, and still others just plain cute. Each member of the family selects their pumpkin. When we return home, we cover the table with lots of newspaper and get to work.

As we cut, clean, and carve we also laugh, tell scary and comical stories and create memories that will last long after the season's pumpkins have rotted. Some years we add painted decorations to the faces or even yarn wigs and hats as disguises. Together, the tradition continues — more for the enjoyment of being together than creating the actual designs.

Yes, I think fall is my favorite time of year. I love the crisp sounds, the brilliant colors, the enticing aromas, the delicious flavors, and the interesting textures. I am thankful for all that I have and hope to share the beauty I have experienced with all interested.

# PREPARING HARVESTED MATERIALS

Throughout the centuries, fall has been the time of year when people have worked most rigorously, bustling to preserve the summer's harvest. It has also been a time of festive celebration and thanksgiving.

It is a perfect occasion to take a walk to gather pine cones, seed pods, fruits, gourds, and berries, along with leaves and flowers for pressing. Children especially love to hunt for these treasures. Their young eyes can spot a variety of objects to use for imaginative designs.

Pick bittersweet while the berries are still yellow. If picked when the berries are red, they will shatter too easily. Pick okra pods before the first frost. Air dry the pods whole or split open so the ends curl into petals. Pick teasels when they are dry on the plant.

Collect cones when they fall from the tree. Wash them in water, using a stiff brush to remove soil if necessary. Bake for an hour at 200 degrees F to give them a shine and remove the pitch. Do not over bake because they will turn too dark.

Hang pods in a well-ventilated area to dry. Bake nuts for 20 to 30 minutes at 200 degrees F to kill insects. Store nuts in cans with a few mothballs to deter mice and other rodents.

Save seeds from pumpkins, squash, watermelon, and beans. Wash seeds and

bake at 150 degrees F for 15 minutes to kill insects and stop germination. In this way, save and prepare pits from peaches, avocados, plums, and apricots.

Harvest gourds late in the season, after the stems have withered and dried. Cut them from the vine, leaving at least two or three inches of stem still attached. Wash in soapy water with 1/2 cup of liquid chlorine bleach. Dry with an old cloth or towel. Hang them by their stems or place them on a screen or rack. Allow air to circulate around them while drying. Wipe off any mold that forms with a damp cloth and a small amount of bleach. If any begin to rot, throw them away. The gourd shell gets very hard as it dries. When it is completely dry it will feel very light and the seeds inside will rattle. Small gourds take up to a month to dry. Larger ones may take six months to a year.

Soft shelled gourds such as the crown of thorns and Turk's turban do not dry well. They provide vibrant color and can be used decoratively for several weeks during the fall season.

Pumpkins are winter squash, though not all are edible. Harvest them before the first frost when the skin has toughened. Interestingly, during the Revolutionary War, soldiers used pumpkins for bayonet practice.

# PINE CONE WREATH

Notice the use of several varieties of cones in this wreath. They are placed right-side-up, upside-down, and on their sides. A few have even been cut in half. We are truly able to enjoy the beautiful textures of pine cones through this design.

## COLLECTING SUPPLIES:

*One 16" (40.6cm) straw wreath form*
*1-1/2 yards (1.37m) of 1-1/2" (3.8cm) wide rust/gold striped ribbon*
*1-1/2 yards (1.37m) of 2" (5.1cm) wide sheer copper wire edge ribbon*
*2 yards (1.83m) of 3" (7.6cm) wide copper mesh ribbon*
*Pine cones and pods: Norway spruce, white spruce, lotus pods, ponderosa (whole and half), red pine cones, jack, white pine cones, black and white spruce cones*
*Glossy wood tone floral color*
*Electric table saw to cut pine cones in half*
*Glue*

*Using all sides of a variety of pine cones creates an interesting look on a Pine Cone Wreath.*

## CREATING THE DESIGN:

To prevent the straw color from showing through between the cones, spray the straw wreath form with wood tone floral color.

To cut a pine cone in half, firmly hold each side of a pine cone and pass it through the saw bottom first. Glue the longer cones, such as the Norway spruce and white pine, randomly around the outside and inside edges of the wreath. Leave room for other cones. Do the same to the top edge of the wreath.

Form a layered bow using the three styles of ribbon. Attach to the wreath. Fill in around the longer cones and bow loops, with smaller and half cones. Entirely cover the wreath.

Use tiny cones such as those from white and black spruce trees to fill in empty spots.

# AUTUMN ILLUMINATION

Imagine rounding the corner through crisp fall leaves on your way to a friend's house for an autumn bonfire party when this spectacular design greets you with its welcoming light and full rich colors. The maple leaves are carved all the way through the pumpkin, while the smaller leaves are merely shaved from the top layer of pumpkin skin. The use of leaves instead of a jack-o-lantern face gives the design a feeling of elegance.

*One large fresh pumpkin, approximately
    12" (30.5cm) in diameter*
*Leaf stencils or patterns*
*12 stems fresh goldenrod — cut 12" to 18"
    (30.5cm to 45.7cm) long*
*12 stems preserved fall oak leaves — cut 8" to
    12" (20.3cm to 30.5cm) long*
*12 stems fresh rust daisies — cut 10" to 14"
    (25.4cm to 35.6cm) long*
*10 stems fresh yellow cushion mums — cut
    10" to 14" (25.4cm to 35.6cm) long*
*10 stems fresh safflower — cut 10" to 16"
    (25.4cm to 40.6cm) long*
*24 stems dried cattails — cut 14" to 18"
    (35.6cm to 45.7cm) long*
*24 stems dried wheat — cut 14" to 18"
    (35.6cm to 45.7cm) long*
*One 6" (15.2cm) round clear plastic
    shallow container*
*1/3 block fresh floral foam*
*Waterproof tape*
*Floral preservative*
*Carving knife*
*Pumpkin carving tool or small straight saw
    blade*
*Single socket light bulb with electric cord or
    large candle*

## CREATING THE DESIGN:

Cut an opening at the top of the pumpkin large enough for the 6" (15.2cm) container to securely rest in place without shifting. Set the top of the pumpkin aside. Scoop out the pulp.

Trace the leaf patterns, including veins, randomly around the outside of the front of the pumpkin. Using a carving knife or pumpkin carving tools, carve the maple leaves all the way through the pumpkin. Shave away the skin for the smaller leaves, leaving the exposed pulp. The deeper you are able to shave without going through the pulp, the more transluscent the light will be. If a light bulb is being used as a light source, cut a hole at the back of the pumpkin large enough to fit the bulb and cord. Choose wattage for the light that will be appropriate for the setting.

Soak the foam in floral preservative-treated water. Use waterproof tape to hold the foam in the plastic container. Create an all-around design with goldenrod, cushion mums, and safflower. Tuck the fall leaves around the base and deep between the flowers. Accent with rust daisies, cattails, and wheat.

Insert several wooden picks in the underside of the cut pumpkin top. Position to one side at the base of the design. The wooden picks will hold the pumpkin to the floral foam.

*Note: Be sure to continually add a great deal of water to this design. The light will dry out the foam and shorten the life of the flowers if not kept watered.*

## GREAT IDEA!

Cut out eyes and a mouth to create a jack-o-lantern. Cut through all the way. Cut a nose and ears partially through the pulp. Insert a heavy stem wire into small chocolate bars and insert throughout the design to add a touch of whimsy and fun.

# BABIES BREATH AND FALL LEAF WREATH

*The Babies Breath and Fall Leaf Wreath combines the delicate look of babies breath with the rustic look of pods, leaves, and gourds.*

The soft delicate nature of preserved babies breath makes it a perfect filler material to use between fall leaves, pods, and gourds. This wreath style depicts the rich abundance of the harvest season.

## COLLECTING SUPPLIES:

*One 14" (35.6cm) straw wreath*
*Two 4 oz. pkgs. preserved natural gypsophila*
*Approximately 50 pressed or preserved fall leaves*
*5 small dried kalabash gourds*
*8 flat protea heads*
*12 clusters dried bittersweet — cut 4" (10.2cm) long*
*30 sweet huck branches — cut 6" (15.2cm) long*
*"U" shaped floral pins*
*3" (7.6cm) wired wooden picks*
*Glue*

*The wreath is first completely covered with clusters of babies breath.*

## CREATING THE DESIGN:

Cut the gypsophila into bunches 3" to 4" (7.6cm to 10.2cm) long. Form small clusters with the bunches. Place the cluster on the wreath and insert a floral pin around the stems to securely hold in place. Attach clusters from the outside to the inside in rows. The next row should cover over the stems of the last row until the wreath is completely full.

Glue the five gourds into a focal cluster. Glue four protea heads into the cluster and equally space the remaining ones all around the wreath. Fill in the focal area with clusters of bittersweet. Glue fall leaves around the wreath, tucking them between the babies breath. Finish the design by inserting huck branches throughout the wreath.

## GREAT IDEA!

Place the wreath flat on a table and use three taper candles in brass candlesticks in the middle to create a striking candle ring centerpiece.

# HARVEST SPLENDOR

I first created this design for a ten city media tour. I presented holiday designs to audiences of morning and noon television shows around the country. In a few cities, the local newspapers were also interested in interviewing me and featuring my holiday designs. This design was the hit of the tour. No matter where I went, people loved it because of its bright colors, interesting textures, and ease of creation.

The unique aspect of the design is that the eucalyptus wreath base can be quickly changed and adapted throughout the year. Use it to create a variety of looks. I have added fall leaves to give the design a bright spark of color. Remove them at the end of the season and the design will still look breathtakingly natural.

## COLLECTING SUPPLIES FOR THE WREATH BASE:

*One 16" (40.6cm) straw wreath form*
*Two 12" x 1-1/2" (30.5cm x 3.8cm) foam discs*
*1-1/2 lbs. preserved brown eucalyptus — cut approximately 5" (12.7cm) long*
*50 pressed or preserved fall oak leaves*
*Sheet moss*
*Two 13" (33cm) long x 1/4" (.6cm) wide dowel rods*
*Floral pins*
*Glue*

*Harvest Splendor combines the beauty of natural materials with the surprise of broken clay pots.*

## CREATING THE DESIGN:

Glue the two discs together on top of each other. Insert the ends of the dowel rods into the inside of the wreath form crosswise. Add glue at the insertion points to secure. On top of the dowel rods, wedge

*The foam is held into the wreath with crossed dowel rods.*

the discs inside the wreath form. Shave the discs to fit if necessary. Glue to hold securely.

Lightly cover the top of the discs with sheet moss, using floral pins to hold in place.

Group three to five stems of eucalyptus together to form a cluster and attach it to the wreath with a floral pin securely pressed over the stem ends. Work around the wreath with the eucalyptus clusters, overlapping slightly to cover the pins, covering the top and outside edge of the wreath form. Insert the fall leaves around the wreath between the eucalyptus clusters.

## AGING CLAY POTS

Saturate the clay pot with soapy water using a spray bottle, allowing the water to run freely. Gently spray with spurts of whitewash, cherry wood tone, brown, and basil floral color sprays. Do not allow to dry between colors.

## COLLECTING SUPPLIES TO AGE POTS:

*Whitewash, cherry wood tone, brown, and*
*    basil floral color sprays*
*Two each 3-1/2" (8.9cm), 4" (10.2cm),*
*    and 5" (12.7cm) clay pots*
*Three 2" (5.1cm) clay pots*
*Spray bottle with soapy water*

## COLLECTING SUPPLIES TO DECORATE CLAY POTS:

*One each 3-1/2" (8.9cm), 4" (10.2cm), and*
*    5" (12.7cm) aged clay pots*
*12 sweet gum balls*
*12 teasels*
*12 stems dried celosia — cut 3" (7.6cm) long*
*Assortment of miniature pods and pine cones*
*3 clusters dried bittersweet — cut 3"*
*    (7.6cm) long*
*3 stems orange dried yarrow — cut 3"*
*    (7.6cm) long*
*6 stems yellow dried yarrow — cut 3"*
*    (7.6cm) long*
*6 stems dried tansy — cut 3" (7.6cm) long*
*20 cattails — cut 10" to 24" (25.4cm to*
*    61cm) long*
*40 stems setaria — cut 12" to 30" (30.5cm to*
*    76.2cm) long*
*20 stems rye — cut 8" to 20" (20.3cm to*
*    50.8cm) long*
*Several short lengths of raffia*
*32 gauge wire*
*1 block dry floral foam*
*Sheet moss*

## CREATING THE DESIGN:

Cut floral foam to fit each of the clay pots and glue inside. The foam should be 1/2" (1.3cm) below the top of the pot.

Form separate clusters of the setaria, cattails, and rye. Near the base of the stems, secure each with a short length of wire. Insert the rye cluster vertically into the foam in the 3-1/2" (8.9cm) pot. Place the cattail cluster into the 4" (10.2cm) pot and the setaria cluster into the 5" (12.7cm) pot. Apply glue around the base of the stems to hold securely. Tie a short length of raffia around each of the clusters to keep the stems from shifting. Lightly cover the top of the foam with sheet moss in each of the pots. Use floral pins to hold in place.

Glue a collection of miniature pods and pine cones, bittersweet, and orange yarrow around the base of the rye cluster. Embellish around the base of the cattail cluster with mini pine cones, celosia, tansy, and sweet gum balls, and around the base of the setaria cluster with teasels, pine cones, yellow yarrow, and celosia.

## RIBBON EMBELLISHMENT

### YOU WILL NEED:

*3 yards (2.74m) of 2-3/4" (7cm) wide wire edge fall print ribbon*
*Ten 3" (7.6cm) long wired wooden picks*

Cut the ribbon into eight 9" (22.9cm) lengths and two 18" (45.7cm) lengths. Form loops using the 9" (22.9cm) lengths. Attach to a 3" (7.6cm) long wired wooden pick. Attach each of the 18" (45.7cm) lengths to separate picks.

## CONSTRUCTING THE DESIGN:

Position the decorated pots on top of the moss covered discs. You may need to move some of the moss aside so that the pots sit flat and do not topple. To simulate a bow treatment, insert the ribbon loops into the disc to the right of the three pots.

Using a hammer, carefully break some of the remaining empty clay pots into pieces and gently place next to and around the decorated pots and ribbon loops.

## GREAT IDEA!

Instead of the decorated clay pots, use carved pumpkins and assorted gourds in the center of the wreath. Embellish with a Halloween print ribbon. The base of the Harvest Splendor design is also perfect to create a whimsical look with jack-o-lanterns.

# ABUNDANT HARVEST TABLE SWAG AND CANDLE HOLDERS

*The Abundant Harvest Table Swag and Candle Holders will enhance the look of any party or celebration table.*

This design was created with freeze-dried fruits and vegetables. The abundance of the season is apparent. If unavailable in your area, replace the pieces with fresh or silk fruits and vegetables. Just be sure to use LOTS — the theme is definitely abundance! The finished raffia swag design is approximately 27" (68.6cm) long.

## COLLECTING SUPPLIES

*An assortment of freeze-dried fruits and*
*vegetables — lemons, limes, oranges,*
*strawberries, quince slices, grapefruit*
*slices, mushrooms, peach halves,*
*eggplant, cauliflower, broccoli, carrots,*
*kumquats, blackberries, potatoes, and*
*mini apples*
*Approximately 40 preserved or pressed fall*
*oak leaves*
*Two 8 oz. pkgs. natural raffia*
*Glue*

## CREATING THE DESIGN:

Carefully open the two packages of raffia. Lay them side by side. Tie, using a double knot, with several lengths of raffia approximately 8" (20.3cm) from the end. Trim the ends even. Divide the bunch into three parts and braid down 15" (38.1cm). Tie tightly under the braid with several lengths of raffia. Trim the ends to a length of 8" (20.3cm).

Starting with the larger elements (oranges, eggplant, potatoes, broccoli, limes, lemons, and cauliflower), glue the fruits and vegetables along the top of the braid. Also glue larger fruits and vegetables along the sides of the braid so that the

design will be pleasing when viewed from all sides.

After gluing a full base of larger materials, fill in with groupings and clusters of smaller materials (strawberries, blackberries, kumquats, mini apples, mushrooms, and fruit slices).

Glue the leaves around and between the fruits and vegetables.

*Braided raffia creates an inexpensive, yet firm base*
*for the Abundant Harvest Table Swag.*

## COLLECTING SUPPLIES FOR THE CANDLE HOLDER:

*One 3-1/2" (8.9cm) aged clay pot — see Harvest Splendor design for aging clay pot instructions*
*One 1" (2.5cm) three-pronged plastic candle holder*
*One 12" (30.5cm) rust candle*
*1-1/2" (3.8cm) x 3" (7.6cm) block dry floral foam*
*Sheet moss*
*Assortment of small freeze-dried fruits and vegetables — blackberries, strawberries, kumquats, mini apples, bits of broccoli and cauliflower, quince, and grapefruit slices*
*Five preserved or pressed fall oak leaves*
*Floral pins*
*Glue*

*Note:*
*Never leave burning candles unattended.*

*Freeze-dried fruits and vegetables clustered around the base of the candle continue the feeling of abundance.*

## CREATING THE DESIGN:

Glue the foam into the aged clay pot. Insert the pronged candle holder into the center of the foam. Lightly cover the foam with sheet moss, using floral pins to hold in place.

Glue the fruits and vegetables in groupings of like materials around the candle holder, interspersing the fall leaves throughout.

# HARVEST SWAG

I designed this swag specifically to accent this incredible log cabin home. The size of the design coordinates perfectly with the surroundings. It includes a large porch with tables and several rocking chairs. The use of colors and textures create a design that is visually compelling to the eye. The sheaf of wheat and setaria appears to extend directly through the center of the creation.

## COLLECTING SUPPLIES:

*(1) 60 stems 30" (76.2cm) long setaria — cut in half*

*(2) 45 stems 26" (66cm) long wheat — cut in half*

*(3) 18 stems red amaranthus — cut 12" to 18" (30.5cm to 45.7cm) long*

*(4) 20 stems hops — cut 12" to 36" (30.5cm to .91m) long*

*(5) 3 thika pods on 4" (10.2cm) long stems*

*(6) 5 poppy heads — cut 10" to 18" (25.4cm to 45.7cm) long*

*(7) 6 proteas on 8" (20.3cm) long stems*

*(8) 3 okra pods on 4" (10.2cm) long stems*

*(9) 3 neri buds on 4" (10.2cm) long stems*

*(10) 12 assorted color dried straw flowers on 8" (20.3cm) long stems*

*(10) 12 stems safflower on 8" (20.3cm) long stems*

*(10) 12 stems stirlingia — cut 8" to 12" (20.3cm to 30.5cm) long*

*6" x 10" x 2" (15.2cm x 25.4cm x 5.1cm) foam block*

*4" (10.2cm) long wired wooden picks*

*One green chenille stem*

*Sheet moss*

*Floral pins*

## CREATING THE DESIGN:

Fold the chenille stem in half and insert both ends through the foam, near the top of the block. Pull until the stem is through the foam. Twist the ends of the stem on the back of the foam to form a loop for hanging the design. Lightly cover the foam block with sheet moss using floral pins to hold in place.

Form clusters using approximately fifteen stems of the cut setaria in each. Attach a wire pick to each of the clusters. Repeat, forming several more clusters with the stem sections and attaching picks to these clusters. Insert into the foam, forming a diagonal line with the stems angling downward.

Repeat this procedure with the wheat, positioning it to the left of the setaria clusters. Position the red amaranthus to the right of the setaria cluster.

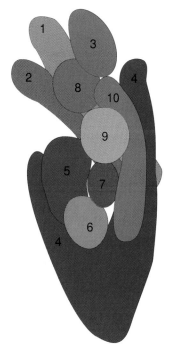

Form a loose oval shaped outline of hops from below the wheat cluster, down, and up and around to below the red amaranthus cluster. The full length of this design is approximately 54" (1.37m). Insert a cluster of thika pods just below the wheat head cluster. Position a cluster of poppy heads and proteas angled downward near the center of the design. Position the okra pods and neri buds angled upward near the center of the design. In the center of the design, fill with clusters of safflower, stirlingia, and straw flowers.

*Be sure to attach the chenille stem near the top of the foam and form into a loop to hang the swag design.*

# DRIED GOURD CONTAINER

The beauty of gourds is that no two are alike. Their size and shape will continue to vary as they grow. When purchasing gourds, look carefully and be sure the one you select will stand on its bottom perfectly balanced. If not, you will have trouble creating a floral design inside.

*The Dried Gourd Container and Bountiful Wheat Sheaf pull their rich colors from the earth.*

## COLLECTING SUPPLIES:

*One dried hard shell gourd, approximately 9" x 7" x 4" (22.9cm x 17.8cm x 10.2cm)*

*26 stems setaria — cut at various lengths 6" to 10" (15.2cm to 25.4cm) long*

*7 stems mini lotus pods — cut 4" to 8" (10.2cm to 20.3cm) long*

*6 clusters tansy — cut 5" to 7" (12.7cm to 17.8cm) long*

*6 clusters celosia — cut 5" to 7" (12.7cm to 17.8cm) long*

*4 natural branches — cut 6" to 9" (15.2cm to 22.9cm) long*

*2 sponge mushrooms*

*Approximately 4 oz. medium gravel*

*One half block floral foam*

*18 gauge wire or 3" (7.6cm) wired wooden picks*

*Spanish moss*

*Small hand saw*

*X-acto™ knife*

*Black marker*

*"U" shaped floral pins*

*Glue*

## CREATING THE DESIGN:

Clean the gourds outside with maximum ventilation. Gourd dust is noxious. You may want to consider wearing a dust mask. If you have sensitive skin or are allergic to dust, wear rubber gloves.

Draw an opening on the gourd with the marker. Score around the opening with an

*First draw the gourd opening with a marker, then use a blade to carefully cut it out.*

X-acto™ knife. Use the saw to finish cutting through the gourd. Thoroughly clean out the pulp.

Cut the foam block to fit the gourd and glue inside. Add gravel around the foam to weigh down the gourd. Cover with Spanish moss and pin in place.

Insert the flowers in groups of like materials. Create four separate clusters of setaria and attach each to a 3" (7.6cm) long wire or wooden pick. Insert the clusters into the foam, creating a diagonal line.

Insert the cockscomb, tansy, branches, and lotus pods in groupings. Place the sponge mushrooms behind the lotus pod grouping.

# BOUNTIFUL WHEAT SHEAF

Wheat signifies "the staff of life," "amber waves of grain," and "bringing in the sheaves," a true sign of the year's harvest. It also expresses good luck and fertility. Create several sheaves of different sizes and display them together on your hearth, front porch, or kitchen counter.

## COLLECTING SUPPLIES:

*Approximately 300 stems 26" (66cm) long blackbearded wheat*
*4 clusters red pepper berries, 5" (12.7cm) long*
*2 flat protea heads*
*3 large pomegranates*
*2 small pomegranates*
*2 dried apples*
*4 dried apple slices*
*Small bunch gold crowsfoot, 5" (12.7cm) long*
*Natural raffia — use nine 48" (1.2m) long strands of raffia to form one braid — make two braids to create braided raffia bow loops*

## CREATING THE DESIGN:

Shape the wheat into a sheaf. Secure tightly under the heads with several lengths of raffia. Cut the stems evenly across the bottom so the sheaf will stand freely.

Wheat is naturally very stiff and straight so the sheaf can look one of two ways. It can look very slender and tall or it can look as the sheaf pictured. Achieve this droopy look by soaking the wheat in warm water for approximately thirty minutes or more if necessary. Shape the wheat to give it a graceful bend.

Glue a cluster of pomegranates and whole dried apples about 6" (15.2cm) below the wheat heads. Shape each of the raffia braids into two loops with two streamers. Secure with a short length of wire. Glue the loops into the center of the cluster. Allow the steamers to hang.

Glue the apple slices around the base of the cluster. Glue one protea head into the center of the loops and the other one angled upward.

Glue clusters of pepper berries and crowsfoot behind the main cluster, forming a diagonal line of materials.

## GREAT IDEA!

Form small wheat sheaves to be used as party favors or individual decorations on a banquet table during the autumn season.

# CORNHUSK WREATH

*The elegance of burgandy and gold combines with the rustic nature of cornhusks, statice, and teasels to create a striking design.*

Cornhusk loops provide an elegant natural base for this wreath design. The rich burgundy and gold tones of the ribbon and leaves are perfect accents along with the interesting textures of the German statice and teasles.

## COLLECTING SUPPLIES:

One 18" (45.7cm) straw wreath
2 lbs. cornhusks
2 oz. package German statice — cut 4" (10.2cm) long
30 teasels — cut 4" (10.2cm) long
30 salal leaves
Burgundy and metallic gold floral color sprays
2 yards (1.83m) 1-1/2" (3.8cm) wide gold striped ribbon
2 yards (1.83m) 2-1/2" (6.4cm) wide burgundy wire edge ribbon
3 yards (2.74m) 2-3/4" (7cm) wide leaf pattern wire edge ribbon
3 yards (2.74m) 2-3/4" (7cm) wide burgundy/gold wire edge shimmer ribbon
Floral pins
Container of warm water
Glycerin
Glue

## CREATING THE DESIGN:

Spray the salal leaves with the burgundy floral color. Gently mist with metallic gold. Set aside to dry.

Soak the cornhusks in warm water with a few drops of glycerin to soften. Fold each cornhusk in half. Pinch the ends of the cornhusk together, place a floral pin over the ends and insert the pin into the wreath, securely holding the cornhusk loop in place. Pin all cornhusks in one direction, overlapping the previous one just enough to cover the pin securing it. Cornhusks tend to shrink slightly when dry so be sure to overlap the pin enough so shrinkage is not a problem. Do the outside and inside edges first, then the top of the wreath form. Leave a 4" (10.2cm) space open on the left side for placement of the bow.

Form a layered bow, using all the ribbons together. Secure the bow to cover the empty space on the wreath. Glue the salal leaves, German statice, and teasels around the wreath between the cornhusk and bow loops.

Soak the cornhusks in warm water with glycerin to make them soft and pliable.

# TIPS

❧ Gild dried gourds, artichokes, and pine cones with a gold or copper floral spray to use for holiday or elegant dinner party decorations.

❧ A basket filled to the brim with an assortment of nuts and cones makes an effective and simple centerpiece.

❧ Dried fruit pits make an attractive addition to pine cone wreaths.

❧ Varnish, paint, or stain gourds for added color.

❧ Dry apple slices in a home dehydrator. To keep the slices white and pliable, soak them for five minutes in a solution of two to three tablespoons sodium metabisulfite F.C.C. and one quart of cold water. Place them in the dehydrator.

❧ To preserve cattails so they do not burst open, cut them before they get soft and stand the stems in a bucket of liquid floor wax.

❧ Prepare fall leaves for use in design by spraying both sides with clear acrylic spray. Spray both sides once, allow to dry, then repeat.

# PART SEVEN
# Techniques

## BOWMAKING

Layered bows, made from several different ribbons, combine to enhance a design. The various widths, color tones, and textures coordinate and add a special touch. This is a challenging bow to create, but can be done if you keep in mind that you are doing one step at a time.

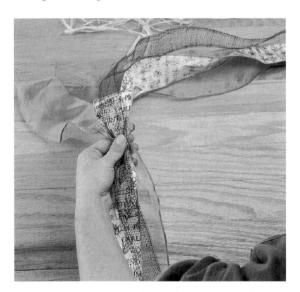

1. I normally use at least three types of ribbon together to form a layered bow. The three choices should vary in color tone, width, and textural quality. To begin, hold all the ribbons together in your left hand (if you are right-handed), between your thumb and forefinger, with the widest ribbon on the bottom and the narrowest on the top. If you are using any additional materials, such as raffia, set them aside for the moment.

2. Pull all the top ribbons toward you and out of the way. Leave only one ribbon with which to work. Keep in mind that even though you have many ribbons in your hand, you will only be working with one style at a time.

3. Form a loop with the ribbon and then pinch the end between your thumb and forefinger. Form a second loop on the other

side of your hand and again pinch the ribbon between your fingers.

4. Allow the first ribbon to lay in its position and pull the second ribbon forward. Form two loops with this ribbon, pinching it between your fingers after each loop. Allow the end of this ribbon to lay in position with the first ribbon.

5. Pull the third ribbon forward and repeat, forming two loops on top of the other loops, pinching the ribbon between your fingers after each loop.

6. While securely holding the loops of ribbon, pull forward the last two streamers that you had laid aside. They should be in the same position as in step 3 — the widest ready to work with, the other two pulled forward and out of the way.

7. Form at least two more loops with each ribbon, following the previous directions. At this point, the bow loops will appear casually mixed up, creating a lovely fullness and texture. You can add as many or as few loops of each ribbon as you like. I love this bow because it never turns out exactly the same. Each is unique and designed to enhance every design individually.

8. I usually add a few extra loops of the top ribbon because it seems to add a softness and a finished look to the bow.

9. After finishing the loops, add any extra materials you wish in the center of the bow. I have added several loops of raffia. Cording, braids, and pearls are a few other materials that are helpful to enhance the look. Hold together firmly in your hand.

10. I usually use a chenille stem to hold the bow together. To keep everything together, a full bow needs extra support and strength. You can also use wire. I prefer cloth covered wire rather than bare wire, again for its extra holding abilities. Place a chenille stem across the middle of the bow.

11. Pull the ends of the chenille stem to the back and twist the ends together tightly right next to the bow. Be sure the twist is tightest directly where the chenille stem

meets the ribbon. Continually twisting the stem further away from the bow does nothing to tighten the core of the bow loops. Accomplish this easily by holding the ends of the twisted chenille stems. Turn the bow a few times.

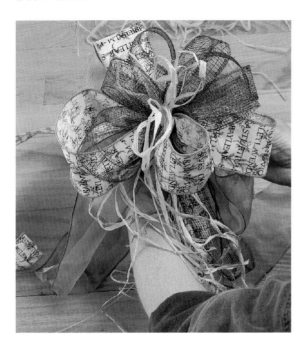

12. When the chenille stem is firmly in place, fluff out the ribbon loops and arrange them so they appear to be casual and random.

## RIBBON LOOPS

There are two methods for forming individual bow loops. These methods are useful in many ways when creating a design.

**Wooden Picks** — A wired wooden pick is a pointed skewer of wood with a wire attached to one end. Bring the ends of the ribbon loop together and pinch it securely, overlapping with at least 1" (2.5cm) of the wired end of the wooden pick.

Wrap the wire tightly around the end of the ribbon and the pick. As you are wrapping, bring some of the wrapping downward to cover the entire end of the ribbon. Allow a few of the wraps to fall below the end of the ribbon and wrap a few times securely around the pick only, then continue back upward, wrapping the entire length of the wire. This helps secure the loop so it will not turn in your design.

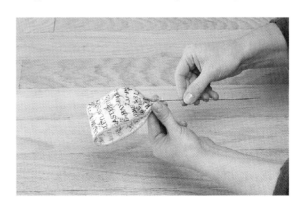

**Wire and Floral Tape** — You can also use a length of 20 gauge stem wire and floral tape to form a ribbon loop. Bring the ends of the ribbon together and pinch securely over the end of a wire, overlapping the ribbon with the wire at least 1" (2.5cm).

Pinch the end of the floral tape around the top of the ribbon and wire. Hold the wire in your left hand with the tape held between the thumb and forefinger of your right hand. Gently turn the stem with your left hand, stretching and wrapping the tape with your right. Tape all the way to the end of the cut stem of appropriate length. Break off the tape and pinch the ends together to secure.

## ATTACHING STEMS

Some natural materials need to have stems attached so they can be inserted and arranged in the design. To do this, hold a length of 20 gauge wire overlapping the end of the item. Pinch the end of the floral tape around the overlapping area to secure. Floral tape is not a sticky tape, it's a waxed crepe paper. When stretched, the warmth of your hands activates the tackiness.

Hold the wire in your left hand with the tape held between the thumb and forefinger of your right hand. Gently turn the stem with your left hand, stretching and wrapping the tape with your right. Tape all the way to the end of the stem.

## LENGTHENING STEMS

Lengthen some stems so that they can be placed in the appropriate location of a design. To lengthen a stem, use a length of 20 gauge wire and overlap the wire and the ends of the stems several inches.

Pinch the floral tape securely with your thumb and forefinger at the top of where the wire and the stem meet. Use the warmth of your fingers on the waxed floral tape to secure.

Hold the stem in your left hand with the tape held between the thumb and forefinger of your right hand. Gently turn the stem and stretch and wrap the tape with your right. The tape stays stationery and wraps as you twist the stem.

## PREPARING CONES AND PODS

To attach a wire to a pine cone, use 22 or 24 gauge green paddle wire and wrap a length of the wire around the base of the cone. Bury the wire deep within the petals of the cone.

Twist the wire ends securely and very closely to the cone itself. Continue to twist the entire length of the wire. For extra holding ability, you can even put floral tape over the stem before insertion.

Using some pods can be difficult if they do not have a wire or stem. In many cases, a stem can be added by using a pointed wooden pick or skewer. Simply insert the pointed end into the end of the pod and add a drop of glue at the place where the pick and the pod meet.

## FLORAL FOAM AND MOSS

There are several types of floral foam available. Use an appropriate arranging foam, as it is crucial to a finished design. Each type of foam suits a particular need.

## DRY FLORAL FOAM

This type of floral foam works well with all types of silk flowers and dried materials. It is a softer foam, so you don't need to reinforce dried flower stems before inserting them.

To determine the size of foam, you will need to cut and measure the foam block inside the container. Place it all the way at the bottom of the container for an accurate fit. For most designs, you will want a small amount of foam to extend above the edge of the basket. Insert flowers parallel to the tabletop or angle them upward into the design. An average measurement of two fingers above the edge of the container is usually sufficient.

After measuring, use a serrated knife to cut the foam to size and shape. Dry floral foam cuts easily.

Securing the foam to the container will depend on the type of container you have chosen to use. If your container is ceramic, glass, metal, wood, or plastic, first cut the foam to fit the shape of the container. Allow some space surrounding the foam (about 1/2" to 1", 1.3cm to 2.5cm), and glue the foam into the container using hot glue or tacky glue.

If you are using a basket with an open weave, sometimes glue is not the best way to secure the foam. After cutting the foam to fit, place the foam in the basket. In three equally spaced locations, insert 2" (5.1cm) long U-shaped pieces of a chenille stem through the bottom of the basket and into the foam.

If the bottom of the basket is extremely uneven, place the foam into the basket and cover it with moss. Insert the end of a piece of flexible wire through the wicker on the basket rim. Twist the end. Repeat on the opposite side of the basket, directly across from the first location. Bring the two wires together and twist them in the center to secure. Trim away all but approximately 1" (2.5cm) of wire on each length. Bend this extra wire under and insert it into the foam. Repeat this process with two wires in the opposite directions so there are four equally spaced wires on the basket.

Cover all dried floral foam with moss so it becomes inconspicuous in the finished design. Spanish moss in its natural color works well. Use sparingly by pulling and spreading the moss to completely cover the foam.

Sphagnum moss works extremely well, also. I like to use this type of moss in its natural color rather than the dyed version. Since it is a natural product, the consistency and quality will vary. To insert stems through the moss and into the foam, you want the moss to be as thin as possible. If the package you purchase is thick and clumpy, pull away any excess bark and dirt from the back.

While holding each side of the moss, rub the backs of the moss together to remove any other thick particles.

Spread the moss over the foam in the container with the moss going all the way down the sides and into the container. Use floral pins to insert through the moss and into the foam to keep it in place.

### PLASTIC FOAM (STYROFOAM®)

Use this firmer foam for silk and heavy-stemmed dried materials. It is available in many different sizes and shapes, in green or white.

To insert easily into this foam, materials with thinner stems need reinforcement with a wired wood pick or a floral-taped stem wire. Secure plastic foam in place with a thick white craft glue, silicone, low temperature hot glue, or craft cement.

### FRESH FLORAL FOAM

This is a water-absorbant floral foam. Use with fresh flowers only. If used with permanent materials, it will soften and fall apart over time. Fresh floral foam holds a large amount of water and is important to the long life of fresh flowers.

The container you use must be able to hold water. Many containers will have a clear plastic liner inside for water retention. If yours does not, you can make a liner yourself with florists' foil. Cut the foil larger than the basket, then place it inside the basket, folding the ends down to secure in place. Some of the foils today are plastic, which is nice because they don't rip or tear as easily as regular florists' foil.

To saturate the foam, use a large container for soaking, approximately twice as tall and twice as wide as the block of foam. Fill the container with water and preservative, following the package directions. Place the foam on top of the water and allow it to submerge.

As it absorbs water, the foam will begin to sink and darken in color. Never push it under water forcefully, always allow it to absorb water at its own rate. Some foams will absorb faster than others — but all take less than five minutes.

Never pour water over the foam block to saturate. Don't make the mistake of thinking that if the entire outside is dark, the foam is fully saturated. When cutting open a poorly saturated block, you will find dry spots in the center of the foam. Stems positioned in those spots will not take up water and the flower will die.

Securing fresh floral foam is a little more challenging because it is wet. If the foam you are using is not too large, you can use hot glue to attach the foam to the container while it is still dry. After the glue cools, then soak the entire container with the block attached. I have never found that the low-temperature hot glues hold very well in this application, especially if the design will go into a refrigerator or cooler. Special fresh floral foam glues are available. Try a local florist or floral supplier.

Complete saturation has occurred when the foam is completely dark in color and only 1/4" (.6cm) of the block remains above the surface. At this point, a full brick of foam has absorbed approximately two quarts of water. When completely saturated, cut the foam with a knife to fit the shape of the container. If the foam fills the container completely, cut a small wedge out of one side of the foam block to allow for addition of water on a daily basis to keep the flowers alive.

The most common method used to attach wet foam is with waterproof tape spread over the top of the foam in a criss-cross fashion and down the sides of the container approximately 2" (5.1cm).

For added protection, place another small piece of waterproof tape at right angles to the ends of the tape on the container. This will help prevent the tape ends from pulling up.

## FLOWER PREPARATION

### AIR DRYING

This is an easy method that allows moisture in plant materials to evaporate naturally. Simply bunch like materials, tie them with rubber bands or string, and hang them upside-down in a dark, dry warm place. Generally, lighter weight materials will take a shorter time to dry than fleshier materials. Most flowers will take at least a week to dry.

Hydrangea, babies breath, heather, and delphiniums dry well in an upright position. Place them in a container with a small amount of water and let the water evaporate. To dry ivy vines, cut long sections after the first frost. Hang the vines in a dark dry spot for several weeks.

To air dry roses, remove them from water when they have reached the full bloom stage. Cut 2" (5.1cm) from the stem, bunch together, tie with a string or rubber band, and hang upside-down in a warm, dry dark space. Apply this method to a variety of flowers and foliage.

### DESICCANT DRYING

To absorb moisture from plant material, use desiccants such as sand, silica gel, cat box litter, and cornmeal. Silica gel, though not the least expensive, is the preferred and only sure-fire method. It quickly removes moisture from flowers and leaves while allowing the retention of color and shape. Always follow manufacturer directions. I recommend using a dust mask when using this product.

Place a 1/2" to 1" (1.3cm to 2.5cm) layer of silica gel at the bottom of an air-tight container. Place the flowers, with the stems cut short or a short wire inserted, upright, on top of the silica gel. Using a large spoon, gently pour more silica gel all around the outside of the flower to completely cover it. The silica gel will mound around the flower, supporting the petals.

Finish covering the flower with another inch of silica gel. The flowers should be ready in one to two weeks. Gently pour off the silica gel. Blow or use a small paint brush to remove particles. Use the silica gel repeatedly. You can even bake it in an oven to dry the crystals out and start using it again. The product manufacturer's instructions will be very clear.

Orchids, daisies, dogwood blossoms, asters, carnations, irises, lilies, daffodils, roses, marigolds, tulips, and zinnias dry well in silica gel.

After drying, store dried flowers in a single layer in a covered container. Shelter from direct light and humidity.

## PRESSING FLOWERS AND LEAVES

Pressing is a simple way to preserve many flowers and leaves. Be sure the plant material is dry. Flowers that contain moisture will not hold their color when pressed. Use only undamaged flowers and leaves. Pick flowers at different stages of development. Press the same kind of materials in the same layer. Flowers with a thick, heavy center do not work as well as those which are flatter. Cut the flower stems close to the head.

A quick and easy way to press flowers and leaves is to simply place a layer of absorbent paper towel on a flat surface and position the leaves and flowers on top. Cover with another layer of absorbent paper.

Use a heavy object such as a dictionary or encyclopedia to keep the materials flat and smooth. Try to find absorbent paper or paper towels that are smooth or have very little weave. The weave design can become embossed in your natural materials during the pressing process. Avoid colored or embossed papers.

Another method is to use a flower press, which you can construct or purchase. To make one you will need two pieces of 1/2" (1.3cm) thick plywood, 8" or 9" (20.3cm or 22.9cm) squares work well, though any size is fine. If you are pressing large leaves, you may want to make your press larger. Drill a hole at each corner 1/2" (1.3cm) from the edge. Use 2" (5.1cm) long bolts and wing nuts to tighten the press.

To set up the press, place a layer of cardboard that has been cut slightly smaller than the plywood on top of the wooden bottom. Lay absorbent paper on top of the cardboard. Cover the paper with as many flowers or leaves as possible without touching. Place absorbent paper on top. Place another layer of cardboard on top of the paper. Continue to fill the press with layers of absorbent paper, plant material, absorbent paper, and cardboard.

Position the wooden top and insert the metal bolts, washers and wing nuts through all the layers of the press. Tighten the wing nuts until the layers uniformly press together. Set the flower press aside in a dry, warm area. Allow seven to ten days for flowers to press and dry. As the flowers dry, tighten the wing nuts so the press remains firmly together.

# MAIL ORDER SOURCES

**Beyond local health food, herb, floral or craft shops, here are mail order sources for some of the supplies in this book.**

**Ferry-Morse Seed Company**
P.O. Box 1620
Fulton, KY 42041-1620
tel. 800. 626-3392
fax. 502. 472-3402
Seeds, plants, bulbs, general gardening supplies

**Shepherd's Garden Seeds**
30 Irene Street
Torrington, CT 06790-6658
tel. 860. 482-3638
Seeds, herbs, spices, general gardening supplies

**W. Atlee Burpee & Co.**
300 Park Ave.
Warminster, PA 18974
tel.  800. 888-1447
fax.  900. 487-5530
Seeds, plants, bulbs, general gardening supplies

**Wildseed Farms, Inc.**
1101 Campo Rd.
P.O. Box 508
Eagle Lake, TX 77434
tel. 800. 848-0078
fax. 409. 234-7407
Wildflowers, regional wildflower mixes, herbs

**Bountiful Gardens**
18001 Shafer Ranch Road
Willits, CA 95490
tel./fax. 707. 459-6410
Heirloom herbs, flowers, books

**Penn Herb Company**
603 North Second Street
Philadelphia, PA 19123
tel. 215. 925-3336
fax.  215.  632-7945
Dried herbs, spices, extracts, oils

**Aura Cacia**
P.O. Box 399
Weaverville, CA  96093
tel.  800. 437-3301
Essential oils, perfume essences

**San Francisco Herb Co.**
250 14th St.
San Francisco, CA 94103
tel. 800. 227-4530
fax. 415. 861-4440
www.SFHerb.com

**Leaman's Green Applebarn**
7475 N. River Rd.
Freeland, MI 48623
tel. 517. 695-4560
fax. 517. 695-4560
Freeze-dried fruits, vegetables, flowers

**More Than A Memory**
6101 Centre Street SW
Calgary, Alberta T2H 0C5
tel. 403. 640-7000
fax. 403. 640-9919
email: goraic@cadvision,com
Freeze-dried flowers

**Kathie's Creative Services**
25 Seville Way
San Mateo, CA  94402
tel. 800. 573-0631
fax. 650. 572-1287
email: kcreate@slip.net
Freeze-dried flowers and fruits

**Monique's Freeze Drieds**
26221 Fifth Ave. NE
Arlington, WA 98223
tel. 360. 435-9706
fax. 650. 572-1287
Freeze-dried flowers, fruits, vegetables, foliage

## For additional floral arranging and wedding floral design books and videos from Kathy Lamancusa, contact:

**Creative Directions, Inc.**
8755 Cleveland Avenue
North Canton, OH 44720
tel. 330. 494-7224
fax. 330. 494-2918
www.lamancusa.com
email - info@lamancusa.com

## For a local garden club branch, contact:

**Garden Club of America**
598 Madison Avenue
New York, NY 10022
tel. 212. 753-8287

# BOTANICAL GLOSSARY

Common names may vary from one region to another. Botanical names remain constant and aid in identification. In the 1700s the Swedish botanist Carolus Linneaeus created the universally accepted system called binomial nomenclature. Linneaeus gave a two-part Latin botanical or scientific name to every plant then known. This classified all plants by their common characteristics into genus and species. Often, all the plants in the same genus will have similar growing and care needs.

The names of hybrid plants are preceded by an "x." This is an exception to the binomial system and is used to name plants that were derived by artificial breeding techniques. The **International Code of Botanical Nomenclature** governs the naming of plants, thus insuring one unique name for each plant.

The first part of a botanical name designates the genus to which the plant belongs. It is always capitalized and in italics. The second part of the name gives the species — a group of plants within a genus that have common characteristics. It is always lowercase and in italics.

**spp.** — Species
**Genus** — A group of closely-related plants containing one or more species.
**Species** — Plants that are genetically similar and breed true to type from seed.
**Hybrid** — Plants with parents which are genetically distinct. The parent plants may be different species, cultivars, varieties or occasionally genera.

African violet  *Saintpaulia ionantha*
Almond  *Prunus dulcis*
Alstroemeria or Peruvian lily  *Alstroemeria* spp.
Amaranthus, "Love-lies-bleeding" *Amaranthus caudatus*
Amaryllis  *Amaryllis belladonna*
Anemone or windflower  *Anemone* spp.
Apple, mini or crabapple  *Malus* spp.
Apricot  *Prunus armeniaca*
Artemisia  *Artemisia ludoviciana*
Aster  *Aster x frikartii*
Avocado  *Persea americana*
Azalea  *Rhododendron* spp.
Babies breath  *Gypsophila paniculata*
Bachelor button  *Centaurea cyanus*
Basil  *Ocimum basilicum*
Bay leaf  *Laurus nobilis*
Bell cup  *Nux vomica*
Bittersweet  *Celastrus* spp.
Blackberry  *Rubus* spp.
Black cherry  *Prunus serotina*
Black-eyed Susan  *Rudbeckia fulgida*
Black spruce  *Picea mariana*
Black walnut  *Juglans nigra*
Blueberry  *Vaccinium* spp.
Boxwood, african  *Myrsine africana*
Broccoli  *Brassica oleracea*
Bronze palm (Fan palm)  *Chamaerops* spp.
Burdock burrs  *Arctium* spp.

Burning bush  *bassia scoparia f. trichophylla*
Butterfly bush  *Buddleja davidii*
Carnation  *Dianthus* spp.
Carnation, white "White Candy"  *Dianthus caryophyllus*
Carrot  *Daucus carota sativus*
Cattail  *Typha* spp.
Cauliflower  *Brassica oleracea*
Celosia "Cockscomb"  *Celosia argentea var. cristata*
Chamomile  *Chamaemelum nobile*
Cherry, flowering  *Prunus serrula*
Chive  *Allium schoenoprasum*
Choctaw foliage (Dogbane)  *Apocynum cannabinum*
Chrysanthemum  *Chrysanthemum* spp.
Cinnamon  *Cinnamomum zeylanicum*
Clematis  *Clematis* spp.
Climbing rose  *Rosaceae* spp.
Clove  *Syzygium aromaticum*
Cockscomb, see also Celosia  *Celosia argentea var. cristata*
Columbine  *Aquilegia x hybrida*
Comfrey  *Symphytum officinale*
Coneflower  *Echinacea* spp.
Corn husk  *Zea mays*
Cornflower  *Centaurea cyanus*
Cotoneaster  *Cotoneaste* spp.
Crabapple  *Malus* spp.
Croton plant  *Codiaeum variegatum*
Crown aster  *Callistephus chinensis*
Crown of Thorns  *Euphorbia* milii
Daisy  *Bellis perennis*
Delphinium  *Delphinium* spp.
Dusty miller  *Senecio cineraria*
Eggplant  *Solanum melongena*
Elderberry  *Sambucus canadensis*
Elm *Ulmus americana*
English ivy  *Hedera helix*
Eucalyptus  *Eucalyptus* spp.
Euphorbia  *Euphorbia* spp.
Fennel  *Foeniculum vulgare*
Fern, leatherleaf  *Rumohra adiantiformis*
Feverfew  *Tanacetum parthenium*
Flowering quince  *Chaenomeles speciosa*
Foxtail fern  *Asparagus densiflorus*
Freesia  *Freesia x hybrida*
Fuchsia  *Fuchsia* spp.
Geranium  *Geranium* spp.
German statice  *Limonium tatarica*
Globe amaranth  *Gomphrena globosa*
Globe thistle  *Echinops* spp.
Gloriosa daisy  *Rudbeckia* spp.
Goldenrod  *Solidago* spp.
Gourds  *Cucumix* spp.
Grapefruit  *Citrus  x  paradisi*
Gum benzoin  *Styrax benzoin*
Heather  *Coluna* spp.
Hedera berry  *Hedera  helix*
Heliotrope  *Heliotropium* spp.
Hibiscus  *Hibiscus* spp.

Holly   *Ilex*   spp.
Hollyhock   *Alcea rosea*
Honeysuckle   *Lonicera*   spp.
Hops   *Humulus lupulus*
Hyacinth   *Hyacinthus*   spp.
Hydrangea   *Hydrangea macrophylla*
Impatiens   *Impatiens*   spp.
Jack pine   *Pinus banksiana*
Jasmine   *Jasminum*   spp.
Joe-Pye weed   *Eupatorium fistulosum*
Juniper   *Juniperus*   spp.
Kiwi   *Achtinidia chinensis*
Kumquat   *Fortunella*   spp.
Lagurus   *Lagurus ovatus*
Lamb's Ear   *Stachys byzantina*
Larkspur   *Consolida*   spp.
Lavender   *Lavandula*   spp.
Lemon   *Citrus limon*
Lemon Verbena   *Aloysia triphylla*
Liatris   *Liatris spicata*
Lilac   *Syringa*   spp.
Lime   *Citrus aurantifolia*
Lobelia   *Lobelia*   spp.
Lotus pod   *Nelumbo*   spp.
Lupine   *Lupinus*   spp.
Mahogany pod   *Swietinia mahagoni*
Marigold   *Tagetes erecta*   spp.
Meadow Mint   *Mentha spicata*
Millet   *Panicum miliaceum*
Ming fern   *Asparagus retrofractus*
Mint   *Mentha*   spp.
Monte casino   *Aster ericoides*
Morning Glory   *Ipomea purpurea*
Moss   *Mnium*   spp.
Mulberry   *Morus*   spp.
Mum   *Matricaria*   spp.
Mushroom   *Basidiomycetes*
Neri Bud   *Protea Nerifolia*
Nigella   *Nigella damascena*
Norway Spruce   *Picea abies*
Nutmeg   *Myristica fragrans*
Oak   *Quercus*   spp.
Oat   *Avena*   spp.
Okra pod   *Abelmoschus esculentus*
Orange milkweed   *Asclepias tuberosa*
Oregano   *Origanum*   spp.
Orientalis   *Nigella orientalis*
Orris root   *Iris florentina*
Pansy   *Viola*   spp.
Papyrus   *Cyperus papyrus*
Patchouli   *Pogostemon patchouli*
Peach   *Prunus persica*
Pennyroyal   *Mentha pulegium*
Peony   *Paeonia*   spp.
Pepper berries   *Capsicum*   spp.
Peppercorn   *Piper nigrum*
Peppermint   *Mentha piperata*
Pine Cone   *Pinus*   spp.
Phlox   *Phlox divaricata*
Plum   *Prunus x domestica*
Pomegranate   *Punica granatum*

Ponderosa Pine   *Pinus ponderosa*
Poppy   *Papaver*   spp.
Potato   *Solanum tuberosum*
Protea   *Banksia coccinea*
Pumpkin   *Cucurbita*   spp.
Pussywillow   *Salix caprea*
Queen Anne's Lace   *Daucus carota*
Red pine   *Pinus resinosa*
Red twig dogwood   *Cornus*
Reindeer moss   *Cladonia*   spp.
Rose   *Rosa*   spp.
Rosemary   *Rosmarinus officinalis*
Rye   *Poaceae*
Safflower   *Carthamus tinctorius*
Sage   *Salvia*   spp.
Salal leaves   *Gaultheria shallon*
Salvia   *Salvia*   spp.
Sandalwood   *Santalum*   spp.
Sarracennia   *Sarracenia*   spp.
Sea grape leaves   *Coccolobis uvifera*
Sedum   *Sedum*   spp.
Setaria   *Setaria*   spp.
Shasta daisy   *Leucanthemum x superbum*
Snapdragon   *Antirrhinum majus*
Spanish moss   *Tillandria usneoides*
Spice bush   *Lindera benzoin*
Spiraea   *Spiraea*   spp.
Sponge mushroom   *Trameles betulius*
Squash   *Curcurbita*   spp.
Star anise   *Illicium verum*
Statice   *Limonium sinuatum*
Stella d'Oro lillies   *Hemerocalis*
Stirlingia   *Stirlingia latifolia*
Strawberry   *Fragaria*   spp.
Strawberry parfait dianthus   *Dianthus Barbatus*
Strawflower   *Helichrysum bracteatum*
Sunny border blue   *Veronica spicatas*
Sunflower   *Helianthus annuus*
Sweet alyssum   *Lobularia maritima*
Sweet gum ball   *Liquidambar styraciflua*
Sweet huck   *Vaccinium parvifolium*
Sweet William   *Dianthus barbatus*
Tansy   *Tanacetum vulgare*
Teasel   *Dipsacus fullonum*
Thyme   *Thymus*   spp.
Ti Tree   *Leptospermum*   spp.
Turks turban   *Cucurbita maxima*
Viburnum   *Viburnum*   spp.
Viola   *Viola*   spp.
Violet   *Viola*   spp.
Watermelon   *Citrullus lanatus*
Weigela   *Weigela*   spp.
Wheat   *Triticum*   spp.
White flowering dogwood   *Cornus*   spp.
White pine   *Pinus strobus*
White spruce   *Picea glauca*
Witch hazel   *Hamamelis*   spp.
Yarrow, yellow   *Achillea filipendulina*
Yarrow, red   *Achillea millifolium*
Zinnia   *Zinnia*   spp.

# INDEX